Smyth & Helwys Publishing, Inc.
6316 Peake Road
Macon, Georgia 31210-3960
1-800-747-3016
©2016 by Rob Lee
All rights reserved.

Library of Congress Cataloging-in-Publication Data

Names: Lee, Rob, 1992- author.
Title: Stained-glass millennials : coincidental reformers / by Rob Lee.
Description: Macon, GA : Smyth & Helwys Publishing, [2016] | Includes
bibliographical references and index.
Identifiers: LCCN 2016049766 | ISBN 9781573129268 (pbk. : alk. paper)
Subjects: LCSH: Generation Y--Religious life. | Church history--21st century.
Classification: LCC BV4529.2 .L44 2016 | DDC 277.3/083--dc23
LC record available at https://lccn.loc.gov/2016049766

STAINED-GLASS MILLENNIALS

COINCIDENTAL REFORMERS

ROB LEE

In his holy flirtation with the world, God occasionally drops a handkerchief. These handkerchiefs are called saints.
—Frederick Buechner

To Bob and Barbara
To Carol and Mickey
To Rusty and Sherrie
To Scott
To Stephanie

You made a difference. Thanks for being handkerchiefs.

ACKNOWLEDGMENTS

Where do I even begin to thank the people who influenced and helped this book come to fruition? Let's start at the beginning: the dedication page. Bob, as my grandfather, you taught me the importance of words in your poetry and musings in your journals. Barbara, as my grandmother, you have been one of my biggest fans and supporters since day one. Mickey, you have always been concerned with my well-being, and your kindness has not gone unnoticed. Carol, you would go to bat for me in any situation, and for that I am grateful. Rusty and Sherrie, as my incredible parents who have guided and directed me from the day I was born, your love and authentic living have shown me the way to a better understanding of myself, of the world, and of Jesus. Scott, my little brother, thanks for being the brother and friend I can always count on.

Stephanie, my beloved, thank you for showing me that love can last and be beautiful and come to fruition in extraordinary ways. Thank you for being there at my lowest valleys and at the mountaintop moments. Thank you for being my light and my best friend. To the rest of the Sansoucy clan who have supported Stephanie and me through the course of our relationship, thank you. I'm looking at you, Ruth, Keith, Kathy, Nick, and Alyssa!

My Statesville crowd: to the congregation of Broad Street United Methodist Church, it is evident the impact you've had on me. From my baptismal cry to now, I cherish every moment. I couldn't have written this book without Mrs. McConnell's English class, where she inspired me to write like there is no tomorrow and reminded me that "half of life is showing up; the rest is committing pen to paper." To the Tsumas family—Harry,

Ellen, English and Anna—who have shown me the heart of God, and to the Perry family, especially Scarlett and Ashlee for being some of my preaching groupies, all I can say is thanks. Molly Wright, my dear high school big sister, has cheered me on and supported me and I am thankful. Jessi Lancaster has inspired me with her talent and grace. Dave, my editor at the Statesville Record and Landmark, gave me a chance in 2011 to be a columnist. Dave, your willingness to take a chance on me was incredible, and I am so grateful. Mrs. Bertha, my confirmation and faith mentor, you are so loved and cherished.

My Appalachian crowd: Dr. Randy Reed, who first inspired the questions about millennials and the church, this book could not have been born without you. Dr. Ammon, who pushed me to apply to Duke, thank you. Natalie Wolf, you have been a steadfast, loyal, and supportive friend in everything I have done. I can't express how important your friendship has been to me. Dr. Katie Adams, the professor who taught me to question everything, you're awesome. Dr. Thomas Ellis, my adviser, who encouraged me when I thought I didn't have what it took to make it out of undergraduate alive, your kindness despite our theological differences will never be forgotten. Dr. Joby Bell, thank you for teaching me liturgy and inspiring me to adore the Widor Toccata. Finally, Chancellor Kenneth Peacock, my first Appalachian friend and chancellor of our fine university during my time there, you changed my life, and for that I am proud to call you friend.

My Duke crowd: Palmer Cantler, I have known you lo these many years, and I am so grateful to have come to know you better during our years here at Duke. Good luck getting elected bishop at twenty-six. Kelli Hitchman, I couldn't have done Duke without you, my friend. You are something else, and you inspire me to be the best Rob I could possibly be; you have quite literally saved my life. Patrick Craig, your intelligence and willingness to be my friend inspires me regularly, and I am confident you will do greater things than anyone at the Divinity School could ever do. Tyler Godshalk, we've been through so much, and your encouragement has left its mark. Dr. Stephen Chapman, thanks for believing in the project. Dr. Hauerwas and Dr. Edie, thank you for inspiring in me to think theologically since the Duke Youth Academy.

Thanks to my First Baptist crowd, especially the youth group I served for two and a half years, for forging me in the fires of vocational ministry. And a special thanks to Mallory and Kelly Vannoy for ministering to me in ways that I am still processing. To the Hartzog family, especially Charles, Mindy, Taylor, and Haylee, thanks for being the best cheerleaders!

To the Gardner and Rousseau families, thank you for being our small-group friends during our time there. To Michele Gardner, thanks for your kindness, support, and friendship! To Grace and Amanda, thank you for your continued friendship. To Evan Owen, thanks for always making me laugh. Thank you to Jennifer Treski for your support. To Ken and Judy, Katrina and Calvin, thank you for adopting me. To Patricia Turner, Caroline Kimrey, and Christopher Langdon, thank you for being wonderful colleagues.

I couldn't have completed this book without the help of the fine folks at Smyth & Helwys Publishing. You dealt well with my anxieties and answered every email I sent (there were a bunch) with patience and kindness. I am especially grateful to Keith Gammons, publisher, who first saw potential in me. I am also grateful to those who contributed to this book in the way of interviews, and to the writers of my foreword and afterword, Bishop Will Willimon, retired UMC bishop and professor of the practice of Christian ministry, and the Reverend Dr. William Shiell, president of Northern Seminary.

Finally, to my clergy mentors in this life who have left indelible marks on my life, the Reverend Rob Rollins, the Reverend Don Shuman, the Reverend Dr. Jason Harvey, the Reverend Nathan Kirkpatrick, the Reverend Dr. Michael Gehring, the Reverend Ned Hill, and the Reverend Michael Lea, thank you, thank you, thank you.

CONTENTS

FOREWORD

Here is a rare thing—a twenty-something who has a good word for the poor, aging, stained-glass mainline church. Rob Lee gives testimony from and to his generation, the millennials, the same folks who gave us the "nones," the believers in "whatever," and the hip generation who has reacted to mainline Protestantism with a yawn accompanied by vast desertions.

What Rob sees when he looks through the windows into his beloved church is a mainline denomination that has been sidelined during his lifetime and is now in grave danger of becoming flatlined, succumbing in great part because of its inability to reach a new generation with the gospel. And yet Rob refuses to give up hope for his church. He is too grateful to the church and its institutions for passing on the faith to him, and too convinced that his church has valuable resources for helping a new generation faithfully follow in the steps of Jesus. Rob is convinced that too few of his fellow young adults know that mainline Protestantism—with its historic stress on thoughtful reflection on the truth of Jesus Christ, its sacramental worship, and its striving to put faith into practice in Christian mission—is the perfect place for equipment in, encouragement for, and sustained living of the Christian life.

When Rob looks at his fellow young adults, he sees a generation with a particular set of challenges and quirks, but he also manages to see those among whom God is moving, working, coaxing, and calling. His book bursts with optimistic, hopeful good news that millennials have a place in the outbreak of the realm of God. "Hey, fellow twenty-somethings," Rob announces, "let me share with you a great gift that was given to me that is meant for you too—the church."

The church may be a gift of God to the millennials, but, as in each generation, it is a gift that needs to be renovated and refurbished. To be a young adult Christian in the mainline today means that one must also become a "coincidental reformer." Many young adults' criticisms of the church are well taken. Rob invites them to step up, take charge, and lead. Whether or not my older generation will be willing not only to invite but also to give authority and power to these much-needed reformers is, for me, one of the pressing questions for church life today. Lord help us if my generation fails to respond positively to this God-given opportunity.

I open the first session of my class on the Theology and Practice of Ordained Leadership by telling the mostly millennial students, "You have a tough job in this class. In order to prepare yourselves for leadership in the church, you need to know what I've learned over the years in my attempts to serve the church. You need to sort through my pontificating and moaning—which typifies the talk of folks my age—and take what you need to be a vibrant church leader in the future. On the other hand, you can't serve the church I served. I have some hunches about the church of the future, but no certain vision. You are preparing for leadership in a very different church from the church that produced most of you. That's not only because cultures change and time moves on but also because we serve a living God, a God of the living and not of the dead, a God with whom we have more future than past. So you have to be willing to roll with the divine punches." I'd say that, from my reading of *Stained-Glass Millennials*, Rob Lee (great student that he is) actually absorbed what I said (an unusual thing among many in his generation!). He has given us a book that shows deep love for the church, particularly in its mainline, Methodist iterations, great wisdom received from his twenty-something years in the church, and great faith in God's future with a new generation of Christians.

Rob Lee's loving, wise, faithful book is a gracious invitation to his generation to make the emerging mainline church the means whereby they live out their faith in Jesus Christ. I hope Rob's invitation will be received by the restless young Christians my church desperately needs in order to be part of God's unfolding future.

—*William Willimon*
United Methodist Bishop, retired, and Professor of the
Practice of Christian Ministry, Duke Divinity School

INTRODUCTION

No storm can shake my inmost calm, while to that Rock I'm clinging.
Since love is Lord of heaven and earth, how can I keep from singing?[1]

If you ever came to my hometown and asked me for a tour, I would gladly give you that tour. I love Statesville, North Carolina, and its people. We'd go to Carolina Barbeque or Mezzaluna II Restaurant, and I'd take you to my home church and other churches in the area that are near and dear to me. Finally, we'd turn down Oakwood Drive and come to an enormous tree that the residents of Statesville know as Moses. I grew up playing in Moses, whose limbs are bigger than most fully grown trees. I'd tell you how my parents and their parents played in this tree. But knowing where this tree is located, you may not even want to get out of the car. Moses sits in the middle of Oakwood Cemetery, a large, rolling cemetery that has grown up around the tree that has been there since before anyone alive can remember. Hold on to that thought as you read.

Have you ever set out on a project and not fully realized where it might lead? I'm not sure I ever set out to write a book like this. Sure, I've always wanted to write a book on theology, so this a fruition of one dream, but a book on millennials? I couldn't have predicted it. This is partly because even the word "millennial" is newer to our lexicon than most words used in theology. Also, I don't identify as well with my generation as others do; it doesn't come easy for me to be a millennial. But maybe that's why I've felt the gentle nudging of the Spirit to take on this project.

It is my hope and prayer that this book, in some small way, will bridge the gap between people of preceding generations and the generation of which I am a part. It is an attempt to be a beacon by which people come to see and know and hear the song in the heart of God. So whether you've seen and known and heard the song for a long time, or this is the first time you have ever joined in the divine dance, you are welcome in the space of these pages.

One night, I was having a conversation with Dr. Diana Butler Bass on Twitter (how very millennial of me), and we came to a profound conclusion together. I mentioned I was writing this book, and I asked her the following question: "When our time is committed to posterity, what do you think will be said of millennials?" Dr. Butler Bass replied, "I hope you save the planet, but no pressure."

The stakes have never been higher in terms of survival for many of the institutions we know as the modern-day church. Some of the iterations of the institution are on life support; still others aren't what they used to be. The prospect of the failing church can truly induce fear. We have enough anxiety to go around as it is. Should we feel the need to pile the church's mess on top of what we're already anxious about?

I'm reminded of a movie that should be required for every seminary student: *Keeping the Faith,* a film made in 2000 starring Edward Norton and Ben Stiller. It's the story of a Jewish rabbi and Catholic priest who are best friends, and both fall in love with the same woman, played by Jenna Elfman. While there is plenty of humor in the movie, there are more serious parts as well. In one scene, the priest, played by Norton, debates leaving the priesthood. He seeks advice from his mentor, who says, "You cannot make a real commitment unless you accept that it's a choice that you keep making again and again and again."[2]

Ultimately, even though the doctors have told us the prognosis is grim, we must commend the institution we know as the church to the love and grace of God. Because the life and death of the institution are in the hands of God, we have to take seriously what the old Catholic liturgy says about the church being present until the end of time. If our Scripture, tradition, reason, and experience[3] mean anything to us and to the church, it is that God has brought forth life from nothing and, more important, life from death. So we are left to share that holy story. We are charged with making the choice to commit to the church again and again and again.

If there is one thing I've learned recently, it's that stories are all we have. We tell our stories because they make up who we are as people, and this is true across generational lines. In those stories, we see traces and hints of the divine dance I mentioned earlier. We see riverbeds where the story was once on fire. Now there remains a gentle yet fervent spark, ready for the winds of God's Spirit to blow.

So I humbly commend this book to you. It is born out of love for the church and for God's people. I am the family member who is not quite ready to begin palliative care. I want to give the church one more shot. I want to give the church the opportunity to feel the winds of the Spirit moving and shaking the old walls of the institution.

I intentionally say that this book is commended to God's people and not just millennials. Though this book is born out of frustration for how the church talks about the millennial generation, I don't harbor any resentment toward the church or prior generational iterations of the institution. It is my hope that this book will be a tool for the Spirit to bring the people of God into a deeper relationship with the Triune God.

As you read these pages, you will find that I love many things, but few rank above Star Trek and cinema. In the 1991 film *Star Trek VI: The Undiscovered Country*, the *Enterprise* is on its last mission. She has faced a changing landscape of culture and practice and has survived valiantly. At the end of the movie, Captain Kirk says, "This is the final cruise of the *Starship Enterprise* under my command. This ship and her history will shortly become the care of another crew. To them and their posterity will we commit our future. They will continue the voyages we have begun, and journey to all the undiscovered countries, boldly going where no man . . . where no one has gone before."[4] Friends, may we be bold enough as the church to head toward that undiscovered country, venturing to places no person has gone before.

Looking back on my childhood, I am thankful that my parents let me play in the cemetery—not only because Moses was the best climbing tree this world has ever seen but because the tree grew in a *cemetery*. Thinking theologically, that's perhaps one of the best places Christians can play these days, because in life, in death, and in life beyond death in the hereafter we belong to God. Won't you embark with me on this story of resurrection and of playing in the cemeteries? "Where, O death, is thy victory? Where, O death, is thy sting?" (1 Cor 15:55)

—Rob Lee, 2016

Notes

1. Anthem by Jeffrey Honore, based on words first published as "Always Rejoicing," by "Pauline T.," in *The New York Observer*, 7 August 1868, and in 1869 published in *Bright Jewels for the Sunday School* by Robert Wadsworth Lowry. Authorship of both words and music is uncertain.

2. *Keeping the Faith*, dir. Edward Norton, Touchstone Pictures, 2000.

3. I am indebted to the Wesleyan Quadrilateral to describe this section.

4. *Star Trek IV: The Undiscovered Country*, dir. Nicholas Meyer, Paramount Pictures, 1991.

Chapter 1

AN INVITATION TO THE TABLE

Wash, O God, our sons and daughters where your cleansing waters flow. Number them among your people; bless as Christ blessed long ago. Weave them garments bright and sparkling; compass them with love and light. Fill, anoint them; send your Spirit, holy dove and heart's delight. —Ruth Duck

I can't tell you the time or date I first heard Ruth Duck's hymn, "Wash, O God, Our Sons and Daughters," but the hymn's words ring true throughout my life and the lives of stained-glass millennials. We are those brought up to be agents of the God who washes and weaves garments for the sons and daughters of my generation. We are committed to the church; we are examples of God's working presence in the world. And we are millennials as well.

Millennials are a ragtag group of people who desperately need a good word from the church of Jesus Christ. We are bound together by our birth years, but we are bound together too by a common identity that involves questioning the status quo, and that means questioning the church.

To best frame this book, I feel that I should frame my own call story. I was forged in the fires of Broad Street United Methodist Church, a downtown community of faith in Statesville, North Carolina. This congregation has nurtured and loved me since I was brought to the waters of my baptism, and I first felt that nagging, sometimes annoying, life-giving call to ministry at Annual Conference a decade ago. I was sitting there with my associate minister, the Reverend Dr. Jason Harvey, at an ordination service at Lake Junaluska (a beautiful place to first feel the presence of God's call on your life). Jason's friend Nathan Kirkpatrick was being ordained that evening in 2006. I had just met Nathan and we had become fast friends.

As Bishop J. Lawrence McCleskey laid hands on Nathan, I felt it. I knew that kind of commitment was for me. I knew deep within my heart that I should give up the salary, the benefits package, the five-year plan I had ready for being a doctor or a lawyer or something else upstanding in society. I knew in those moments of ordination that God had ordained for my life to follow a similar path.

I have served and preached in small churches in tiny hamlets and in large churches in my state's largest cities. I have had the opportunity to teach and preach and center myself in the church—a gift that millennials often don't have. People seem afraid to hear what millennials have to say about the church, so there is considerable hesitancy to allow someone like me to speak in a church setting.

I must confess that I haven't always wanted to pursue my call after that night in the mountains of Western North Carolina almost a decade ago. I knew I was going to go to seminary (preferably in the land of the Duke Blue Devils), and I knew God had called me to the life and work of a minister. There have been incredible ups, and there have been dastardly downs. But the hope of resurrection then and there and here and now has kept me centered.

That's what this book is about. It is a book of resurrection. Stained-glass millennials, as I am calling them, are people born between mid-1980s and the mid-1990s who have chosen to stay in the institutional church. For a variety of cultural reasons, millennials are least likely to attend church and are less religiously oriented than previous generations.[1] The reality is that we can no longer say that millennials will inherently come back to church as they age, even though many of their parents did.

This book is the alternative to that narrative. It seeks to explain the realities of our time while saying that there is another way. It seeks not to romanticize the stories of those who stay but to show that there is another way to do church in the twenty-first century. There are people who aren't leaving the church, and their stories are beautiful. Though their numbers may be smaller than the droves that have left the institutional church, it is my hope that I can articulate that leaner doesn't have to be bad. In fact, it can put the church in the position where our Lord calls us to the margins to be with those who need the church most.

Church is not what it used to be. In the 1950s and 1960s, people lived, breathed, and ate at church. Now, churches are closing their doors because of financial trials, membership and attendance decline, and the deaths of members who gave most of the support. The church is ailing, but we should take this reality as a challenge to show who we are and whose we are. We must articulate ourselves in different ways and means.

I can vividly remember an encounter I had on Facebook. I was scrolling through my feed, and all I saw were posts about the reasons the millennial generation is leaving the church. We could go into the reasons, but the point is that everyone is convinced that millennials are gone for good in regards to the church. Part of me wanted to comment on every single status and say, "What about me? What about my friends who are attending seminary? What about the group of laity I know who are young and committed to the work of the church?"

This book is born out of that frustration. You could tell me until you're blue in the face that I am the exception to the rule, and I realize that may be the case. But I also know that the entire biblical story is filled with exceptions to the rule. Much of Christian history is an exception to the rule. That's how the church and the forefathers and mothers of the Christian faith operated for centuries before the church came to control the status quo. The future of the church is vastly different than what some people imagine, but the future of the church is bright.

Stained-glass millennials are a determined bunch who seek to articulate that the way to the hope of resurrection lies in the future of the church. They are people who are giving their vocational livelihoods to the church, even if the church doesn't always want them to have a space at the table. It is my hope that after reading these pages, you will have a deeper understanding of why some millennials are choosing to stay—and why that is so important.

I'm not saying that the future of the church rests only on millennials; in fact, it's quite the opposite. We are called into community across generational lines, and, frankly, millennials like myself need community. With community comes accountability and understanding of our limitations. For the time being, many millennials buck at these ideas. As with generations before them, they believe they are inheriting a bygone system, and the flagship of that system is the church. So what can the church do to change? How can the church begin a conversation that welcomes millennials?

Years ago when I felt called to ministry, I had no idea what that would entail. I had no idea that the church was falling apart and that it might be better for me to serve in a healthier institution. But God doesn't need a pulse to make life happen in the church. God can bring back from death and the brink of death the institutions that further the kingdom of God here on earth. God is going to use the millennial generation in incredible ways, and these stained-glass millennials are people you need to meet and get to know.

I can remember God speaking to me at the moment of ordination for my friend Nathan like it happened yesterday, and my goal is simple: I want people to experience that same awe-inspiring, God-filled, heart-warming moment in which grace is undeniable because we have experienced it time and time again. For even as I wavered in my vocational call, even amid doubts of faith, I have experienced God's grace upon grace. I have found that God is ever and always bringing God's people to God's self. It is in that spirit that the church will have to change.

The promise of the twenty-first century is that church can be done differently, better, and hopefully more righteous in its context. The love of God is reaching across our globe, and millennials who stay in church experience that love and open themselves to sharing it with others. As you read these stories of people who stay in the church in spite of their generation, I challenge you to consider why *you* stay (or perhaps why you left). Consider your own narrative and why the church has meant so much to you. If you do this, you will begin to see that God is at work and working still. God is not done with the church yet, and I think the evidence is found in stained-glass millennials. Resurrection can happen, even for my generation.

As a millennial, I invite you into this conversation. I invite you to witness the work God is doing in and through millennials who stay in the church. I invite you to sing that hymn, "Wash, O God, Our Sons and Daughters," in the hopes that God will continue and bring to completion the good work God has started in the millennial generation.

Note

1. J. M. Twenge, J. J. Exline, J. B. Grubbs, R. Sastry, and W. K. Campbell, "Generational and Time Period Differences in American Adolescents' Religious Orientation, 1966–2014," PLoS ONE 10/5 (2015).

Chapter 2

WHY STAINED-GLASS MILLENNIALS?

We have ventured worlds undreamed of since the childhood of our race; known the ecstasy of winging through untraveled realms of space; probed the secrets of the atom, yielding unimagined power, facing us with life's destruction or our most triumphant hour. As each far horizon beckons, may it challenge us anew, children of creative purpose, serving others, honoring you. May our dreams prove rich with promise, each endeavor well begun. Great Creator, give us guidance till our goals and yours are one.[1]

On the first day of lecture in my ordained leadership class at Duke University Divinity School, we were posed the question, "Why are you buying stock in a dying organization?" It's true: the church isn't what it used to be. Is the institutional church heading the way of the buffalo or Blockbuster video? These questions must be faced in our time and place because, as at any pivotal time in the church's history, the church must decide how to respond with what has been placed before us.

Millennials are an interesting breed. One source for the term "millennial" is William Strauss and Neil Howe's book, *Generations: The History of America's Future, 1584–2069*. While the exact years of birth vary for millennials, the generation consists roughly of those born from the years of the 1980s up to the end of the twentieth century. Strauss and Howe later published a book titled *Millennials Rising: The Next Great Generation*. In it they wrote,

> As a group, Millennials are unlike any other youth generation in living memory. They are more numerous, more affluent, better educated, and more ethnically diverse . . . . Over the next decade, the Millennial generation will entirely recast the image of youth from downbeat and alienated

to upbeat and engaged—with potentially seismic consequences for America.[2]

Going deeper than that, it is obvious that religiosity in the United States and elsewhere has been on a downward spiraling trend. According to a Pew Research Center article in 2012, "One-fifth of the U.S. public—and a third of adults under 30—are religiously unaffiliated today, the highest percentages ever in Pew Research Center polling."[3] The article goes on to say that those who are not religious now don't care to be religious in the future. "The unaffiliated say they are *not* looking for a religion that would be right for them. Overwhelmingly, they think that religious organizations are too concerned with money and power, too focused on rules and too involved in politics."[4] That's a hard reality check for the institutional church today. It's not easy for us to realize that we may need palliative care in the near future. But while the results of the Pew Research Center don't lie, I feel like they offer a narrative that is not the whole conversation of the institutional church today.

The Reverend Dr. James Howell, senior minister at Myers Park United Methodist Church in Charlotte, North Carolina, wrote an article in *The Charlotte Observer* apologizing for the institutional church "We believe some beautiful, energizing, healing things about God," he wrote, "but sometimes we come off as dogmatic, wielding a Bible as if it were a weapon instead of a window into the heart of a good God. Or sometimes we are just plain boring. For this we are sorry."[5]

I echo Dr. Howell's sentiment. I also suggest that the church is listening to a narrative that society is forcing upon it. Yes, our numbers are down and finances are not good; that much is true. There is, however, an alternative narrative being lived out by a smaller but more invested group of millennials who are living out their vocational identities in the institutional church. This book, then, is one part call to action and one part storytelling. In it, I seek to tell the story of millennials who are investing in an organization many consider to be dying. Let me lay out a roadmap for how this book works and why it is important. Within these pages lie story after story of an alternative narrative that could be useful for the church and its mission.

How the Book Is Laid Out

CALL TO ACTION

This book is an attempt to call the institutional church to action. The church is a beautiful, life-giving force if done right. I want to see church done right by millennials. I want to see the institutional church valued by baby boomers and others in such a way that it is worth an investment by millennials. We can only accomplish this reality by reforming, reshaping, and resurrecting the values and realities that make the church unique. If we don't do that, we will fail and become just another nongovernmental organization.

We must seek to be like reformers in centuries past. We must celebrate the beauty of the church while challenging the status quo that has made it comfortable. The old saying goes, "We must challenge the comfortable and comfort the challenged." That reality goes a long way for the sake of the church. I look to John Wesley, a reformer not by choice but by circumstance, and feel that millennials who are invested in the church are not trying to be reformers, but simply by their presence, theology, and ideals, are reforming the church in beautiful ways. The circumstance remains, and the choice is ours. How will we respond to this call to action by the millennial generation?

STORYTELLING

I am not the only voice in this book. As a person called to congregational ministry, I believe that I am called to be a storyteller as a subsection of my vocational identity. I've spent years in my short life as a columnist and as a writer and as a preacher, telling the sacred story I believe to be true for the church. But I am just one person. So I've done something dangerous and edgy for the sake of this book and for the sake of the church: I've asked other millennials to tell their stories. Throughout this book, you won't just hear about my theology of reformation. You will also hear reflections from stained-glass millennials who desperately believe that the church still has hope. I've given them questions to guide their reflection, and at the end of each reflection are questions their stories raise that might be able to help you on your journey toward reformation. You'll hear from the vast beauty of many traditions and ways of theological thinking. All we have are our stories, and I hope the stories shared here will be meaningful for you.

Reality Check

The reality is that I don't want to call for a reformation. I love the church the way it is and the way it has been over the past fifty years. It has nurtured and called me in ways I never thought possible. But it is precisely because of that calling and nurturing that I felt I must write this book. It is my attempt to say to the church that it has so much to live for if it will come to the realization that it has hope. Reformation is born out of hope. I won't say the reformers of old always had it right, nor am I saying I or my colleagues in this book have it right. But we're on to something here if you'll give millennials a chance.

In the end, it is up to the church. The church must decide its worth—not society, not financial implications, not dwindling attendance, not the researchers who have given the church palliative care. If it wants to survive, the church must decide its worth. Institutionally speaking, financial realities and obligations aren't necessarily fatal for the church. The church must be the one to carry its own banner forward into the future.

You might ask what's at stake. What difference does it make? Many have said, as the Pew Research indicates, that the church is not concerned with what really matters. Though that may be the case in many instances, we have the weight of 2,000 years of history behind us. Every time Christians engage with millennials, they are effectively determining the future of the institutional church. The relational aspect of the church must never be neglected.

Change We Can Believe In

In 2008, I was too young to vote. I believed so earnestly in the work and political ideology of then Senator Obama that I drove people who couldn't drive to vote so that I could play a small role in the Obama campaign. His campaign slogan was "Change We Can Believe In." Regardless of your political ideology or persuasion, the Obama campaign resonated with many voters, and his campaign of reform and change won him the White House.

What "change we can believe in" is found within the church? How can the church inspire and create passionate and devoted parishioners of the millennial generation? This book will address the reforming and reshaping of missions, sacraments, worship, following Jesus, and church membership. Doing this will take serious considerations and possibly even concessions from the present power structure, but our understanding of history and theology tells us that all are linked together in the body of Christ. That means the future of the church is bound up both in the generation leading now and the millennial generation learning to lead.

Change we can believe in and get behind is what the church needs. We need to believe that Jesus meant what he said when he stood in the synagogue in Nazareth and read from the prophet Isaiah, "The Spirit of the Lord is upon me, because he has anointed me to bring good news to the poor. He has sent me to proclaim release to the captives and recovery of sight to the blind, to let the oppressed go free, to proclaim the year of the Lord's favor" (Luke 4:18-19). This is the church's opportunity to proclaim the year of the Lord's favor. We do so by reclaiming and reforming what it means to be a Christian in the twenty-first century. We live in an incredible time of opportunity to be a person of faith, and we must not take it lightly.

What we say and do matters. People are watching those of faith with great anticipation and curiosity. When our time is committed to history, how will the church fare? Will we be the ones who bring fresh expressions of God's grace and hope within the walls of the church? The reality is that time will tell, but we cannot rest on our laurels and hope for the best.

The Reverend Ned Hill, retired senior pastor of Edenton Street United Methodist Church in Raleigh, North Carolina, once told me that when he is done with his appointment at that large downtown church, he doesn't want to be able to say, "Well, it didn't get any worse." He wants to grow, to change, to shape the church for the future. Will you be content with, "well, the church didn't get any worse," or will you seek the change we can all believe in?

An Invitation to Discipleship

Ultimately, this idea that we have the potential to change is an invitation to discipleship. For in discipleship, we are called to change. Whether that is casting our nets on the other side of the boat or realizing that a thief can enter paradise, we all have the potential to shift the trajectory of our reality. We do that through the grace of God, and we go forward in that hope.

Will you join in the discipleship of the institutional church? Will you fight for the institution that we have grown to love over the years of our lives? If so, how will you begin this journey of discipleship? Let me suggest one idea. There's a beautiful prayer practice where you start out with your fists clenched for three minutes, followed by letting go of the clenched fists and raising your palms to the sky. These motions simulate and give depth to the idea of letting go of what binds us and receiving what God has to offer us through the hope of the future.

This book is not an attempt to give you the answers; it is not an attempt to solidify the future of the church. This idea that millennials are still invested in the church is an invitation for you to let go of the clenched fists of institutional drama and decay and open your palms to the heavens to receive what God has in store for the church. We're all in this together, and we share the beauty of discipleship with one another by growing together.

This means making some concessions and having some hard conversations. But nowhere in Scripture are we promised that the life of faith is easy. I am only reminded in these moments of the words, "He will never fail you nor forsake you" (Deut 31:6).

The Promises this Book Claims

In John's Gospel, Jesus says to his disciples,

> I have said these things to you while I am still with you. But the Advocate, the Holy Spirit, whom the Father will send in my name, will teach you everything, and remind you of all that I have said to you. Peace I leave with you; my peace I give to you. I do not give to you as the world gives. Do not let your hearts be troubled, and do not let them be afraid. (John 14:25-27)

Stained-glass millennials claim the promise of Pentecost. We ask that the Holy Spirit would descend and rest on our bodies, as the Spirit often does. Stanley Hauerwas and Will Willimon wrote in their book *The Holy Spirit*,

> Christianity is a historical reality. The historical reality of Christianity is not just that the church has a history, but rather that our God actually showed up in history. God, thank God, refuses to leave the course of human history up to humans alone. Even as the Holy Spirit takes up space by resting upon bodies, so the Holy Spirit is the typical, continuing way that the Trinity is made known in time.[6]

For us, and for the salvation of the world, the Spirit is working, moving, and breathing within stained-glass millennials, these beautiful young people who choose to stay in the church. It is the church's job to cultivate and help resonate the notes that bring about the Holy Spirit in the lives and vocational identities of millennials committed to the church.

This book claims the promise for Gentiles as well. You heard me speak of millennials within the church, but what about those we haven't reached or have reached unfaithfully? Let me explain. In Acts, Peter realizes that the Holy Spirit is being poured out upon the Gentiles, a group of people originally thought to be excluded from the Messianic promise. Peter returns to Jerusalem and is questioned about his encounter with the Gentiles who received the Holy Spirit. He responds, "And I remembered the word of the Lord, how he said, 'John baptized with water, but you will be baptized with the Holy Spirit.' If then God gave them the same gift he gave us when we believed in the Lord Jesus Christ, who was I that I could hinder God?" (Acts 11:16-17).

After the crowds hear, they are silenced and realize what has just happened. They say, "Then God has given even to the Gentiles the repentance that leads to life" (Acts 11:18). My hope is that this generation that has been disenfranchised by the institution in so many ways can claim the promise to the Gentiles. While millennials may not always have the answers to their questions, may the church be brave enough to sit with them in their doubt. And while millennials may question the way things have always been done, may the church rest in the unchanging grace of God offered from generation to generation, to Jew and Gentile, to baby boomer and millennial.

It is my prayer that millennials will no longer be the subject of church consulting firms or focus groups but instead included in the beautiful tapestry of the institutional church. May we no longer be test subjects or remedies for a dying church but instead an integral part of the kingdom of God.

Going on to Perfection

When I served at First Baptist Church in West Jefferson, North Carolina, I preached a sermon on perfection. After worship, an exasperated parishioner said to me, "You talk a lot of perfection, as if you expect that I'm supposed to be perfect. Well, I can assure you I'm not." I later called that parishioner and reminded them that while I know it's a tall order to be perfect, it's exactly what I expect to happen for each of us in this life. You see, I was formed in the Wesleyan Tradition, and John Wesley fervently believed that we were going on to perfection of love in this life. It is our goal, our hope, our mission to meet that perfection with open arms.

The idea that millennials matter for the existence and future of the church is not a new one, but the idea that we can go on to perfection together with all sorts of generations might be. Many have already written the church off, for church people are too political, too angry, and too quick to judge. Won't you soul search with me? Won't you see what stained-glass millennials have to offer the church?

What would resurrection look like for the church? It would be a reformation, a reframing, a reshaping, a reigniting of epic proportions. We would find ourselves deeply invigorated by the work of the Spirit in our lives and the lives of our faith communities.

Ultimately, stained-glass millennials are people who have been lost but not in an existential sense. These people I encountered and whom you will soon come to know are lost in a different way. As Charles Wesley penned, "Finish, then, Thy new creation; Pure and spotless let us be. Let us see Thy great salvation perfectly restored in Thee; changed from glory into glory, till in Heav'n we take our place, till we cast our crowns before Thee, lost in wonder, love, and praise."[7] Let's get lost in the world of millennials so that we may be lost in the world of where Jesus calls us to go.

Notes

1. Catherine Cameron, "God Who Stretched the Spangled Heavens," Hope Publishing Company, 1967.

2. Neil Howe and William Strauss, *Millennials Rising: The Next Great Generation* (New York: Knopf Doubleday Publishing Group, 2009).

3. Pew Research Center, "'Nones' on the Rise," 9 October 2012, http://www.pewforum.org/2012/10/09/nones-on-the-rise/ (accessed 17 October 2016).

4. Ibid.

5. James Howell, "We Christians Have Harmed, and We're Sorry," *Charlotte Observer*, 23 January 2016, http://www.charlotteobserver.com/opinion/op-ed/article56113305.html#storylink=cpy (accessed 17 October 2016).

6. W. Willimon and S. Hauerwas, *The Holy Spirit* (Nashville: Abingdon Press, 2015).

7. Charles Wesley, "Love Divine, All Loves Excelling," in *Hymns for Those that Seek and Those That Have Redemption in the Blood of Jesus Christ*, 1747.

Chapter 3

REFLECTIONS FROM THE STAINED GLASS

with Steven Coles

The God who I serve, worship, and hope others find is raw, bruised, and bleeding. One who wears a crown of thorns rather than jewels. A God who does not leave while I am in pain, but knows and feels with me. Our will God sit with us in Sheol. —Steven Coles

Steven Coles is a witness to the faith, a person who has been to the depths of hell and found God there. When I first asked to interview Steven, I didn't realize the implications for him or for this book. Then, as he was submitting his answers, Steven said, "The God I serve, worship, and hope others find is raw, bruised, and bleeding. One who wears a crown of thorns rather than jewels. A God who does not leave while I am in pain, but knows and feels with me. Our will God sit with us in Sheol."

Steven is an example of the immense harm the church can do, but he is also an example of the great and mighty grace of God in our lives. I'm honored to know Steven, and it's humbling to share his story here. It is my prayer that you will glean from him that God is not about calling the qualified but qualifying the called.

A second year master of divinity student at Duke University Divinity School, Steven is currently doing a field education assignment at a church in Durham, North Carolina.

Rob Lee: Tell me how you were called to the ministry.

Steven Coles: I have always struggled to answer this question. To start, I did not grow up Christian. I mean, my family and I attend Easter and Christmas programs, and I sometimes attended my grandparents' church. But God did not mean anything to me. When I was twelve, my mother's health declined rapidly, and I thought she was going to die. After a few conversations with people in my hometown, and gaining a basic understanding of Jesus, I thought I would give the church a chance to change my life for the better.

At sixteen, I accepted Christ as my Savior in a small Baptist church where I worshiped and attended youth group. Eventually, the church became smaller and the youth group dwindled. My best friend was in another youth group in town at a Nazarene church. I thought that would be the next best thing, so I started to attend. I became a member, sang on the worship team, and helped out with the youth group. I made plenty of friends, and I hung out with these friends—or whom I *thought* were my friends—outside of church. One of them raped me. Out of fear for my and my family's safety, I kept silent about what this person did to me. I still attended church and high school with this person.

We actually sat next to each other every Sunday, and every Sunday my heart broke. One Sunday, the pastor was preaching on love. I do not remember quite what he was saying, but I knew I needed to pray. While the pastor was preaching, I went to the altar and just listened. Eventually, I began to think, "I could talk about love and God's love to other people." I soon blocked out that passing thought as my hurt bubbled back into my head. I began to curse God. Then I stood up and went back to sitting with my abuser.

Eventually, I found myself at the closest Nazarene school, studying philosophy and religion with some of the best people in the world. During that time, I was working on my personal health and working to do well while at university. During this time, as a part of my healing process, I began to talk with licensed professionals about my sexuality. By the end of my junior year of college, I had come out as gay to a select few people. Shortly thereafter, I left the Nazarene church because I didn't feel welcomed. I stayed away from the church for months and gave it little thought—until a professor, who attended a United Methodist church in town, told me about the church and how accepting it was. I decided to go and I never looked back. To answer your question, I do not know why or how I was called. I just felt drawn to the church. Singing, working with youth and children, and even just being with people drew me into the church. I am only in the church because of the grace of God, and I hope that others can see and feel that same grace from God by things that I do in the church.

Why buy stock in a dying organization? That is to say, why are you pursuing a calling that many millennials and people your age have given up?

To be honest, I hate this question. This question assumes a lot about the church. Primarily, it takes a capitalistic model and equates members of the church to numbers on a graph. I do not see beauty in numbers, but in people. Even if the church has one person in it, it is beautiful. But I'll answer the question: I primarily work with youth and children. I have taught, preached, even sung in front for kids and teens a number of times in my short life. All I can say is that, if we think the church is a "dying organization," we have a poor view of the future for our children. For example, I am a big crier. I will tear up at the sight of a butterfly sometimes. There is something beautiful when you see an infant being baptized or see a teen accept Christ. If we, the church, can continue to fight for the church and seek Christ, even for one child or teen, then the church is not dying. It is truly thriving. Sure, the number of Christians is dropping in North America and Europe. But the church is still growing in other places around the world! It will continue to grow if we keep putting stock into our future, which I believe to be in the hands of our children.

How has your calling affected your relationships, friendships, and family dynamics? Are your loved ones concerned that you're interested in a precarious ministry? What is your response to them?

Like I said before, my family was not primarily Christian. When I told my dad I was studying philosophy, he had a few words of warning for me. When I told my family I wanted to be a pastor, it had almost a similar shock factor as when I told them I was gay. More than anything, my family has supported me in everything I do and have done. My family does not fully understand what this life of ministry might hold for me, but I am in that boat with them. I do not know what my life will look like in five or even ten years. Following the will of God is never certain, but I am not alone in this journey because I have my family and friends who are with me—worries and all.

Where have you seen God in the millennial generation?

Bars, the grocery store, even on the street corner. The church has moved beyond the building and is now outside. That is not to say there is no place for the physical church. I have read a couple of books that state that most millennials are moving back into the four walls of the church (*You Lost Me* by David Kinnaman and Ally Hawkins). There is a want and a need for the church, and millennials have tried to find the church in other places. I fully believe that God is in those spaces too. I have had encounters with people in these spaces, and I have felt the Spirit moving there, even when I have talked with a drunk person about Jesus. God is outside; we just have to be willing to go find God in spaces and people where we would least expect God to be. For example, I was at a bar one evening where a band sometimes plays hymns (among other worship-like songs). It was during this time, over a beer, that I was able to talk with a man about Jesus and why I was at seminary, all while listening to a band play "Come Thou Fount of Every Blessing." It was a holy moment in a place that has been seen as unholy.

What gives you the most hope about the church?

CHILDREN! I cannot stress this enough. If we have any future, it is in our children. Jesus was explicit about children in the Gospels, and I think that was for a good reason. We, as Christians, are supposed to have child-like faith (Matt 18:2). How can we know what that faith looks like if we are not engaging with our children? We need to be actively involved with children, especially in church—teaching, leading, and exploring things like the worship service and helping our children grow and seek the love of God in all things.

Why stay? Why now? Why be a part of this movement that is slowing down?

The short answer: I do not know. I have been hurt greatly by the church, and I am still hurt by the church. I see greatness and love in the church too. That always outweighs the bad that the church does. I have hope and see the church being what it is supposed to be: a sanctuary. I often find myself watching Disney's *The Hunchback of Notre Dame* just to hear Esmeralda sing her song, "God Help the Outcast." Oddly enough, it gives me hope that one day people will not have to think twice about running into a church and feeling safe. In fact, I hope people will seek the church for that very reason and feel safe. It is a lofty goal. We might not be able to be achieve it because we are human. But God is working and redeeming all, and I think that means the church too.

What are your hopes for the future of the institutional church?

I hope and pray every day that the church can be a sanctuary. A place to question and wrestle with anything. A space where we can talk about topics like sex in a more robust way. A place where we can better explore and work for justice. A place that will love better each and every day. I pray that the church, in all of its parts, will work for the coming kingdom of God and not be afraid, even if that means being uncomfortable. I want the church to be a sanctuary because, for me, it has not been, but the church has not always been what it is supposed to be. With continued violence, bigotry, racism, sexism, and the high rates of sexual abuse, the church is nowhere on the radar of places for people to flock to when they need sanctuary. I wrote a blog titled "Sometimes Pastors Wear High Heels." I wrote it as a reflection on working in a shoe store while also working at a church. I saw how much that shoe store could be a sanctuary for so many, but I did not see that all the time at the church I worked for, and it broke my heart. We, the church, need to strive to seek God with all that we are and pray for the church to be what the church was meant to be—and that is a sanctuary.

REFLECTION QUESTIONS

- How can the church better engage with and involve children in God's kingdom?
- How can we make the church a sanctuary big and wide enough for all of God's beloved children?
- How have you been hurt by the church? How has God begun to heal your wounds?

Chapter 4

CALLED TO MINISTRY IN PRECARIOUS TIMES

*"I hear you are entering the ministry," the woman said down the
long table, meaning no real harm. "Was it your own idea or were you
poorly advised?" And the answer that she could not have heard even
if I had given it was that it was not an idea at all, neither my own
or anyone else's. It was a lump in the throat. It was an itching in the
feet. It was a stirring in the blood at the sound of rain. It was a sick-
ening in the heart at the sight of misery. It was a clamoring of ghosts.
It was a name which, when I wrote it out in a dream, I knew was a
name worth dying for even if I was not brave enough to do the dying
myself and could not even name the name for sure.*
—Frederick Buechner[1]

As he often is, Frederick Buechner was on to something in the quote above.
Many people, if asked why they enter the ministry, give a muddied answer
because our vocational paths and trajectories are muddied. But is that such a
bad thing? We were created as creatures who live our lives with a clamoring
of ghosts behind us and a lump in our throats as we go forward. We are
called to ministry in precarious times. We are called for a moment that the
church has not witnessed in a long time, a time where trust in the institutional church is down and attendance is declining.

I've already noted that church attendance is on a steep decline toward
zero. Churches are dying in numbers we hadn't conceived, and most millennials want nothing to do with a dying civic club or community organization.
Ultimately, for many, that is what the church has become: a nongovernment
organization that is vying for money. I am tired of that tale. I am tired of
that narrative. The church as I know it can be alive and vibrant if given
the right tools and resources. One of those tools is vibrant, alive, on-fire

millennials who are passionate about God's grace present in their lives. We share this passion best through telling our stories.

We are called to ministry in precarious times, but we are called nonetheless. We are not the church of the 1950s or 1960s; we are the church of the twenty-first century, which can be more daunting than trying to be vibrant and authentic. Writer and theologian Diana Butler Bass puts it this way:

> A recent survey from Public Religion Research discovered that the majority of churchgoers in the United States express high levels of both nostalgia and anxiety. By strong majorities, religious Americans—particularly white Protestants, and without any significant difference between theological conservatives and liberals—believe that "our best days are behind us" and that the future of society is bleak. In particular, mainline congregations are caught between valorizing the good old days and a deepening sense of desolation that some promised future will never arrive. Evidently, most Protestants would rather look back with sadness than trust that a more just and beautiful future beckons.[2]

Could this be true? Are the best days of what we know as church behind us? If this is the case, why is God calling people like you, me, and countless others to a lifetime of ministry? I think, in some regards, we are missing the point.

The point of the church in the millennial age is not to be a building in the center of town with two worship services that are meant to meet everyone's needs. If we are called to ministry in precarious times, then the church must serve in precarious positions. We must serve on the margins with the people with whom Jesus identified, the people to whom he ministered.

I love the story of Esther in the Old Testament. This iconic biblical heroine realized that, in her day and place, she was meant "for such a time as this" (see Esth 4). But Mordecai had to say that to her before she was able to recognize the potential suffering of her people. Have we, like Esther, become content? Have we become blind to suffering? If so, the church has a lot more to work out than attendance decline or institutional trust.

That clamoring of ghosts that Buechner was talking about is a heavy mantle for any generation to carry. But millennials are desperately trying to figure out if the mantle is worth it. We are called in precarious times, and sometimes the costs outweigh the benefits in ministry. In a cost-benefit consumerist society, ministry becomes even more precarious.

Even so, I am hopeful. I am hopeful that God will bring to fruition vocational callings in the lives of young millennials and bring fulfillment to the vocational callings of preceding generations. The interconnectivity of the church and life itself is striking. We build on the vast canopy of saints who have woven a tapestry for us to continue. When millennials gather together, worship together, and pray together with other generations, the ministry to which we are called becomes real and alive. I believe that the current generation has much to learn in the coming few decades as the torch is passed our way.

Are Millennials Ready for the Precarious Church?

While many of my peers along with myself are realizing a call to vocational ministry or identity within the church, the question must be asked: Are millennials ready to receive the torch passed on to us from preceding generations? I think the answer has the potential to be a resounding yes. The reality is that millennial leaders in the church must pursue opportunity and leadership in the church because they are no longer the future. They are the very real present of the church and must be treated as such. Their callings and vocational identities must be honored. Their sacred worth as children of a living God must be brought to light. In this mindset, we go forward as a church, hoping that God will do God's best work when it comes to the millennial generation.

Let me be clear that the future of the church never rests on one generation alone. But rarely does so much rest on the future of the institutional church as it seems to here and now. The millennial generation is called in a time that presents the opportunity to join the ranks of the great reformers of the church, from Luther to Calvin to Wesley. Who will be the next shapers and reformers of the church? It is my belief that if millennials are given a chance to shine with the light of Christ, then they will shine with a surprising intensity. This has the potential to be a time of spiritual and religious awakening in our world. The institutional church must capitalize on this moment with millennials or risk losing everything the church holds dear. But the church must also be willing to give up some things for the sake of the future of Christ's church.

Here and now, millennials are called. Some millennials are called to the sacred order of ministry, and some are called to be faithful laity. Some millennials are spending their time in the great seminaries of our country, and others are pilgrimaging across this world to find their place in the church. Regardless of situation and circumstance, the church can no longer rest on the realities of previous generations.

Give Us a Chance

Some of you may be wondering, what if millennials don't want the mantle of the institutional church? We must all ask ourselves this question. But this book is an attempt to show that there are millennials across North America who are committed to preserving the institution that we so desperately love. In my own calling and vocational identity, the people who have mattered most have been those from generations prior to mine who gave me a chance and fanned the flame of the Spirit within my soul. These were people who lent their ear and their pulpit, their kindness and their clout to support my work and ministry.

Millennials need to know, as I have come to know, that there is a place at the table for us. There is also great potential for leadership and responsibility. The Reverend McKennon Shea, current major gifts officer at Duke Divinity School, served as director of admissions at Duke Divinity while I was in college. Over the course of his time in that role, he read what must have been thousands of applications from millennials where they recounted the significant moments in their call to ministry. One day over lunch, he and I had a conversation that struck me as something we could all process and put into action. Shea said that there are several kinds of "calling experiences" that people my age need to cultivate if we want to continue having first-rate students at institutions across the country.

The first experience important in deciding to pursue a vocation of ministry is a mission trip that brings the students close to the heart and mission of God. I will cover this more in the chapter titled Engaging Millennials, but how might we begin to focus on being missional toward the community in which we live and work? How can millennials play an integral role in reaching out to those around us?

The second experience Shea suggested as key to the formation of a clear vocational identity is campus ministry in high school and college. If you think back on your own journey, you may realize that for many of us, college or campus ministry was important and imperative to our formation as faithful disciples of Jesus Christ. For me, at Appalachian State University in the Blue Ridge Mountains of North Carolina, the Presbyterian-Episcopal Campus Ministry provided innumerable friendships and countless experiences that formed and shaped me into the person I am today.

The final experience Shea offers is internships and opportunities offered by the local church. For those of you in full-time vocational ministry, think back on your life and trajectory of ministry. Who allowed you a chance to preach? Who didn't? How did they influence you for better or for worse toward who you are today? These opportunities at the local church level are a necessity for one's call as a minister. Again, in my life, Broad Street United Methodist Church let me intern during my senior year of high school. That experience was forming, shaping, and affirming. If the church can create spaces like that for generations to come, we will be safely in line with what God calls us to do. There are some wonderful lines in 1 Kings 19 where Elijah throws his mantle over Elisha and calls him to be a disciple (see 1 Kgs 19:19-21). Who has thrown their mantle over you? Who will you cover with your mantle?[3] Millennials need a mantle and a mandate from the church. Millennials are bent on a mission, and the church will benefit by creating and encouraging opportunities for them to serve.

But Even if Not

In my humble millennial opinion, the Reverend Dr. Samuel Wells is one of the greatest preachers in the world. Dr. Wells was dean of Duke Chapel and is currently vicar at St. Martin-in-the-Fields in London. A few years back he preached a sermon to a crowded Duke Chapel for the Divinity School's baccalaureate service. The sermon was titled "But Even if Not," and it told the story of Shadrach, Meshach, and Abednego in the fiery furnace from the book of Daniel.

Dr. Wells eloquently goes through all the situations of a future minister's career and paints a picture that even if we give up, God doesn't. Dr. Wells preached,

> Maybe you'll flourish in ministry; maybe you'll have a clear sense of call and that call will be honored and fostered by disciples and overseers alike. Maybe every day you'll wake up and feel a freedom in God's service that surpasses any other possible joy. But even if not, know that God is redeeming the world through your hands, your feet, your heart, your love, your gentleness, your kindness, whether you're aware of it or not.[4]

Sam Wells is on to something too. Millennials may be nervous about our abilities, our insecurities, and our downfalls, but God can redeem and restore and use even the millennial generation, a generation that many have given up on. If millennials have a God who believes in us, who works through us, and redeems even us, then what can't we accomplish?

Redeeming Millennial Callings

I had a friend in high school like none other. Her name was Abbey Tsumas, and I cherish our unique friendship to this day. I vividly remember one day when we were part of Leadership Statesville, a community effort to develop young leaders to make a difference in our city. We had the opportunity to go to an art gallery and listen to a presenter talk about the importance of art. I had just turned seventeen, so while that may sound enticing now, I wasn't a bit interested. Instead, I convinced Abbey to do what good students like us should never do: skip and get a bottled Coke with me at the café on the floor below. It sounded like a good enough idea to her, so we left and went downstairs. As any good skipper of class knows, you eventually get caught—and caught we were—but we laughed that day like very few other times in my life. We reminisced and talked future plans. I recall her insisting that I would officiate at her wedding one day when a lucky guy came into her life.

But Abbey died the next week. I remember where I was, what I was doing, and how I felt. I was just recovering from a period of darkness in my life with my own health, so knowing that she had died was crippling in every way. Even more crippling was my doubt and my disbelief in any god or any entity that would take Abbey away from us. I had to bury my disbelief and doubt, however, and preach her funeral. To be completely honest, her funeral restored my faith in the most unlikely of ways.

I am a manuscript preacher. I preach from a manuscript, and I plan to do so for the rest of my career. That day, I had a nicely prepared manuscript to preach, and preach I did. More than one thousand people heard my sermon that day at Abbey's funeral. But what was interesting was what they heard. I had the manuscript ready, but at one point I veered away and mentioned that I was doing the wedding Abbey had always wanted me to do after all. That day, at her funeral, she was married to Christ for eternity. I don't know what it was about that line, but I do know it resonated with people—and with myself—in ways I never thought possible. The Holy

Spirit infused grace into that moment, and, in one off-the-cuff remark, a disciple of Jesus was born anew in the waters of his baptism.

The sure and certain hope we can take away from this is that God will redeem and restore even the most damaged callings millennials have. God restored me. God will restore you. God will take the mess we've made collectively and the mess we've made on our own and bring new life from the bones of death. The millennial generation's doubt in the institution or even in God may not be a bad thing. As a friend often tells me, "We doubt, and doubt, and doubt. But then, if but for a moment, we experience the divinity of God."

It would be awful for us to have it all figured out as twenty-somethings and thirty-somethings. What joy would we have in growing older or discovering anew the God of love, grace, and hope? Let us linger in the doubt for a while, for doubt is the birth pang of redemption. Doubt gives way to the glorious sunrise of resurrection.

Called and Not Forgotten

Millennials are called to the work of church. But some things will have to change for this church business to work in the twenty-first century. The remaining chapters offer ideas for reforming and reshaping the church in ways that might give more access to a generation desperately in need of Christ and Christ's church.

We in the institutional church, from baby boomer to millennial, realize that something is terribly wrong. But just because something is wrong doesn't mean we can't fix the problems we face. Just because we are a broken institution doesn't mean God can't do God's best work in and through us. I love the old saying, "God has not brought us this far to leave us here alone." For we have a sure and certain hope that God comes to us in life, in death, and in life beyond death. Even if that death is of the institutional church as we know it, God is waiting to raise to life a generation of leaders. Millennials, like generations before them, are beautiful, irreplaceable icons of a loving and living God. Millennials deserve to be treated as such. If we start treating each other with an *imago dei* theology—that is, with the idea that we all have the image of God instilled in us—the world will look a little different, the church will look a little different, and we will go forth into the world knowing that God goes with us.

Take Heart

A wonderful story in Mark's Gospel speaks to the reality of being called in precarious situations. Blind Bartimaeus has become one of my favorite biblical characters thanks to a sermon James Howell preached. In the story, Jesus is on his way to meet his destiny in Jerusalem when he comes to Jericho. As Jesus passes through, blind Bartimaeus, son of Timaeus, is on the side of the road. When he realizes that Jesus is coming by, he yells, "Jesus, Son of David, have mercy on me!" The crowd is flabbergasted that this beggar is calling out to Jesus, so they order him to be quiet, which only fuels his desire for mercy. He cries out even more loudly, "Son of David, have mercy on me!" Jesus, filled with compassion, says, "Call him here." The followers of Jesus call to Bartimaeus in a way that is remarkable.

In his sermon, Dr. Howell pointed out that they don't say, "The Messiah is wanting to fix your problems and your past." They don't say, "Jesus is about to instate universal healthcare. Don't worry! You will be cared for." What they do say is, "Take heart, get up, he is calling you" (Mark 10:46-52). Bartimaeus regains his sight and follows Jesus along the way.

The hope of this story is not in the miraculous recovery of sight for one man. The hope of this story is that we can take heart because Jesus is calling us. We can take heart and follow Jesus because countless saints have done just that over a vast swath of this earth's history. For two millennia, we have found ourselves called by Jesus to be more than we are now. That is the hope millennials can have, and that is the hope the church can share with them.

Take heart, he is calling you.

Notes

1. Frederick Buechner, *The Alphabet of Grace* (New York: HarperCollins, 1970).

2. Diana Butler Bass, "The Power of Today" (sermon), *Day1*, 24 January 2016, http://day1.org/7044-the_power_of_today (accessed 17 October 2016).

3. I am grateful to Dr. Renita J. Weems, theologian, who helped flesh out this idea in my mind.

4. Sam Wells, "But Even if Not," sermon, Duke University Chapel, 12 May 2012, https://chapel.duke.edu/sites/default/files/May12ButEvenifNot.pdf (accessed 17 October 2016).

Chapter 5

REFLECTIONS FROM THE STAINED GLASS

with Rhody Mastin

We must honor our stanzas for they are beautiful. We must honor our stanzas for though their rhythm is slow, they are not yet finished. And we must honor our stanzas for they are ours, and that is enough of a reason to stay. —Rhody Mastin

Rhody Mastin has one of the brightest minds I have encountered across my time at divinity school. Her gifts and graces for academia have not gone unnoticed by many of her peers (myself included). But her story is remarkable because she is a millennial who has found the life-changing love of Jesus Christ through her interactions in community and through her intellectual ability to analyze the beauty of what God is doing in her life and the life of the church.

Rhody is an example from the Cooperative Baptist Fellowship that God is breathing new life into a "denomi-network" that is only a couple of decades old. Born in reaction to the fundamentalist takeover of the Southern Baptist Convention, the Cooperative Baptist Fellowship works to acknowledge the service of both women and men in ministry. It is through this lens that Rhody goes about her ministry and her calling. I am grateful to know her and thankful for her investment in the church.

Rhody Mastin is currently a second year divinity student at Duke University Divinity School.

Rob Lee: Tell me how you were called to the ministry.

Rhody Mastin: The moment when I submitted myself to my "calling," I was sitting in the balcony of Fredericksburg Baptist Church during a Mother's Day service. My pastor preached about God's *hesed*, the Old Testament Hebrew word that describes God's love as faithfulness and loyalty. He spoke of *hesed* as something almost bodily: "down in our bones . . . a reverberating sound: *hesed, hesed, hesed, hesed.*"

To be sure, this was not a moment that felt particularly saturated with *hesed*—it was actually quite the opposite. I felt my "calling" as an isolating experience. I didn't know how to label it as a "calling" in any explicit sense, and, in turn, it was difficult to talk about. And it was also not a moment in any brief sense of the word. I had felt impulses of that saccharine term "calling" for many years, but as I sat in my home church's sanctuary on Mother's Day, hearing the articulation of calling as *hesed* triggered something, indeed, within my bones. I prefer to think of my "calling" as my *hesed*: it is within my bones like spongy marrow, in my blood like sticky thrombin. To deny God's *hesed* in my life would be to deny my own substance.

As my pastor said in that sermon, "All the paths of the Lord are *hesed*." In the church balcony I realized, with a comforting sense of claustrophobia, that I would not be able to go where God was not already going. I wanted to take this seriously, and I suppose that could be my answer to how I arrived at divinity school. But it is also about my recognition that no matter what profession I end up in, there is *hesed*. I carry it within myself, and it has transformed my understanding of what ministry is and how we participate in it through daily, mundane, ordinary acts of faithful action.

Why buy stock in a dying organization? That is to say, why are you pursuing a calling that many millennials have given up?

As a member of the Cooperative Baptist Fellowship, I committed myself to the church upon my profession of faith and baptism at age thirteen on Easter Sunday. That is to say, one of my denominational perks is that I remember my baptism quite vividly. When I've considered that I might be better off without the church, remembering the sensation of my wet, braided hair—dripping with baptismal waters—against my Easter dress has been enough to call me back to my physical need for the church.

There are some holy things, quite simply, that one cannot get outside of the church. While I can drink wine in community with friends and call it fellowship, I cannot access the sanctified blood of Christ at any old vineyard. While I can bake bread with my grandmother and feel that these moments with her are sacred, I cannot partake of the body of Jesus in her kitchen. And while I can marvel at how clean and renewed I feel as I step out of the shower and call the sensation a moment of grace, I cannot baptize myself. There are moments of fellowship, sacredness, and grace throughout our daily lives, and for these moments, thanks be to God. But I do not believe that these moments are substitutionary for church and the ways we are blessed specifically through it.

And if it is indeed, as you say, a dying organization, then I will sit by her bedside as she moans in pain. I will wear my Easter dress to her funeral and attend with wet, braided hair so that I will feel in all of her looming dampness what she has done for me.

Where have you seen God in the millennial generation?

As a Baptist, I have a strong conception of the priesthood of all believers. That is, I believe in your ability to be my minister and my ability to be your minister. I believe that we are each capable of serving each other holy wine and Barefoot wine, and that there is something sacred in the various acts of Communion and community we share. Being able to see my friends—even the atheists who are annoyed when I explain this to them—as my priests shifted the paradigm a bit. God is present in my generation as God has been present in every generation before mine and will be after mine. I say with reverent honesty that I have never been left wanting for God's presence in those around me. While I sometimes yearn for churches that feel authentic, I witness the authentic God in those around me each day.

What gives you the most hope about the church?

Last summer I worked as a worship leader for a youth camp. The overall theme for the summer was "Revolution," and one particular day of camp had the theme "stand." On "stand" day, the worship service was especially important to me. Because the theme of the day was "stand," at the beginning of the worship service I would invite campers and chaperones to briefly stand up if there was a moment that resonated with them or declared something that they personally believed to be true. We wanted to reinforce the idea that "standing up for something" required actual movement of our bodies.

I was always a bit nervous about how campers and chaperones from various church backgrounds would receive this instruction. It was a relatively unusual worship practice, so I was worried that asking campers to stand during worship would make them feel uncomfortable or awkward.

But I was wrong. At one point in the worship service, our camp pastor preached on gender equality in the church. He got a little fired up, walked to the edge of the stage, and declared, "Girls, you can preach!" When I was planning out this worship service, my hope had been that a handful of people might stand up at this point in the service to show solidarity with women. Granted, the campers in attendance usually came from liberal Baptist churches and were used to seeing women in the pulpit, so our pastor's statement may have seemed too obvious to warrant standing.

But after a long moment of silence, five little girls, maybe ages eleven or twelve, stood up so quickly that you could hear the sound of their seats smacking the back of the auditorium chairs. You could hear their jeans rubbing against the velour of the seat cushions as they pushed themselves onto their feet. And then you could hear the holy seat slaps all around as the whole congregation stood up in solidarity and agreement.

The image of standing has provided me with great comfort when I ponder the state of our churches. Young women and men who are willing to move their bodies to show what they care about prove to me that we cannot definitively call the church a dying institution. Indeed, the image of the young girls standing reminded me that even if the church is a dying organization, Jesus reminds us ever still, "*Talitha cum*" ("Little girl, get up!").

Why stay? Why now? Why be a part of this movement that is slowing down?

Why stay when it's slowing down? Oh, there is beauty in the slowing down. Perhaps contrary to your thesis intent, I do not always think that slowing down implies death, or that slowing down is inherently bad. Indeed, only by slowing down can we attend to the complexity of our narratives of church, faith, and growing up.

In a lecture Diana Butler Bass gave in 2013 at the University of Virginia titled "Leaving Church? Generation Next and the Future of Faith," she explained that the narrative of the millennial generation and church can be characterized by progress just as easily as it can be characterized by decline.

But to mark our relationship with church so unilaterally ("It's great! We're moving it forward!" or "It's so sad. Nobody is in church anymore.") is to forget about the poetic form our history takes. She argues that each generation must be allowed to contribute its own stanza to the church's poem. There is no "last word" in this poem—there is no death of the church or finite understanding of "slowing down."

We must honor our stanzas for they are beautiful. We must honor our stanzas for though their rhythm is slow, they are not yet finished. And we must honor our stanzas for they are ours, and that is enough of a reason to stay.

REFLECTION QUESTIONS

• In your own life, how are you honoring the stanzas Rhody talks about?
• What moments have reminded you of Jesus' words, *"Talitha cum,"* which mean, "Little girl, get up"?
• How can we enact moments of *hesed* in the twenty-first-century church?

Chapter 6

WHY FOLLOW JESUS NOW?

Millennials and the Problem of Religious "Nones"

We meet you, O Christ, in many a guise; your image we see in simple and wise. You live in a palace, exist in a shack; we see you, the gardener, a tree on your back. In millions alive, away and abroad; involved in our life you live down the road. Imprisoned in systems, You long to be free; we see you, Lord Jesus, still bearing your tree.

We hear you, O Man, in agony cry; For freedom you march, in riots you die. Your face in the papers we read and we see. The tree must be planted by human decree. You choose to be made at one with the earth; the dark of the grave prepares for your birth. Your death is your rising, creative your word: the tree springs to life and our hope is restored.[1]

I never had the kind of conversion experience Paul has in Acts 9. There was no blinding light, no blindness gifted with sight, no miraculous experience. I find myself more in line with Timothy, who was raised in the faith by his mother Eunice and grandmother Lois (see 2 Tim 1:5). Regardless of whether I had that saving experience with a laser show to complement it, I am convinced that Jesus is Lord. God will bring to completion the work he started in us through Jesus for the sake of God's kingdom. I am confident that the God who created me is revealed through the person of Jesus of Nazareth and is best brought out in the faith we know as Christian.

But I may be an exception to the rule in terms of my proclamation among the millennial generation. According to the Pew Research Center,

> Religious "nones"—a shorthand we use to refer to people who self-identify as atheists or agnostics, as well as those who say their religion is "nothing in particular"—now make up roughly 23% of the U.S. adult population. This is a stark increase from 2007, the last time a similar Pew Research study was conducted, when 16% of Americans were "nones." (During this same time period, Christians have fallen from 78% to 71%.) Overall, religiously unaffiliated people are more concentrated among young adults than other age groups—35% of Millennials (those born 1981–1996) are "nones."[2]

A significant number of my peers no longer acknowledge the God who created them and called them into being. This is unfortunate, but I believe the battle for the sake of my generation is far from over.

This chapter seeks to reinvigorate the message of Jesus for a millennial generation. There are no fancy three-step programs to getting your millennial saved—just hope-filled observations about what Jesus can and will do in the lives of millennials.

What Would Jesus Do?

Ask any person in my generation if they wore a "What Would Jesus Do?" or "WWJD" bracelet, and the answer, regardless of where they stand now, probably would be yes. Those bracelets took over the 1990s and early 2000s, and though they were a staple for evangelical Christianity, I think we might be able to glean something from it.

What *would* Jesus do? Maybe more important, what would Jesus *not* do? The Jesus I have come to know would be appalled at today's political climate and might even work to dismantle it. The Jesus I have come to know would welcome the stranger and immigrant, the "other" and the "none" alike. So if Jesus would welcome everyone, why can't Christ's church do the same?

I think millennials and even preceding generations have forgotten the power that the church could wield for the good of the world. Instead, we're consumed with issues of sexuality and finance, of who's in and who's out. We'll cover that in a later part of this book, but the reality needs to be spoken here: the power of the church is being squandered for infighting over

issues that are not the forefront or mission of the gospel. For this life-changing love of Jesus Christ, a love that brings a different light to all the issues
the church could ever squabble about, is the forefront and point of Jesus'
incarnation, crucifixion, and resurrection.

The question "what would Jesus do" may have in fact ruined a
generation. For we have answered the question incorrectly. We have boxed
Jesus up and put a bow on him to make him more palatable for our
twenty-first-century sensibilities. We have made Jesus into something of
a fairy-tale character that caters to what we need along with the needs of
others who look like us. Instead, if we viewed Jesus for who he really is, a
dusty first-century Palestinian Jew who was almost thrown off a cliff for
what he said in Luke's Gospel, we might find ourselves treating each other
differently and taking better care of our world. If we followed that Jesus,
then millennials might get behind what we know to be true about God.

Do You Hear the People Sing?

Les Misérables is one of my favorite musicals. I've had the opportunity to see
it multiple times, and the movie version with Anne Hathaway is stunning.
But I didn't know about the beauty of this musical until my band teacher
shared the book and the original Broadway cast video with me back in my
middle school days. I came to know the musical through my band teacher
in middle school. Likewise, we come to know Jesus through relationships.
It is a beautiful gift that has the potential to be an awful curse.

I hear it all the time: people are hurt in relationships. Christians hurt
people. What is scary is that sometimes the victims believe they are irrevo-
cably damaged by what the church has done to them in the name of Christ.
Whether by a rush to judgment or exclusion from the community, the
church can do terrible harm toward people who might be considered outside the mold of the church. Dare I say we are too consumed with "reaching
perfection in our ranks" than loving and living like Jesus?

If we're serious about reclaiming the millennial generation for the sake
of the church and the gospel, then we must be willing to admit that we
have failed miserably. Christianity, after all, has its roots in failure. Sam
Wells writes,

> The symbol of Christianity is a man dying alone in agony, rejected by the
> great many and abandoned by the close few. Christianity is founded above
> all on the forgiveness of sins, which is something you only get to dis-

cover the day you have the courage and the humility to say "I realize I've been wrong and I've failed and I'm sorry." Christianity is like a 12-step program: you only get to be part of it if you're prepared to say the terrifying words "I have failed."[3]

For those outside the walls of the institutional church, we must be willing to sing the song of failure and grace, doubt and hope. This song of failure and grace is a far different cry than the one many churches are singing now. For the song of Jesus is one of failure and grace, but many churches are too consumed with the song of hypocrisy, greed, and judgment. If we're going to continue to talk about Jesus, we'll have to relearn and reform what it means to talk about him as his disciples.

Reforming How We Talk about Jesus

If religious "nones" are on the rise, then the church must begin to change the language of how we talk about Jesus. For the past century, it has been acceptable to use "churchspeak" to describe the life and times of Jesus of Nazareth, the person we know as the Messiah, but the world is shifting and changing drastically. That being said, we must work to reform how we talk about Jesus with care, because we cannot forsake the message for the sake of the audience.

If we want to reform how we talk about Jesus, we need a back-to-basics approach of theological thinking that doesn't abandon our theological moorings. We must not dismiss the teachings of Jesus that look vastly different from the tendencies of people in American society. Jesus was, after all, a first-century Palestinian Jew who would probably have condemned much of the empire the church has built today. If that is the case, then the church's getting back to the basics is less about attracting followers of religion and more about a mandate from Jesus to be followers of the way he described in his life, death, and resurrection.

Even so, religion was Jesus' stomping ground. As a religious person, he sought to reform the way religious and nonreligious people thought about God. If this becomes the church's mission, then we are surely destined for greater things. Because people are desperate for a good word about the Creator of heaven and earth, they intrinsically crave the hope of God's promises to God's people. The church must stand in the gap, talking about Jesus in such a way that attracts people to the message of Jesus. That is no small task.

Take Up Your Cross and Approach the Text

If we want to make Jesus' message attractive, then we've got our work cut out for us. Jesus said things like, "If you want to follow me, take up your cross and deny yourself" (Matt 16:24). He didn't mince words, and he often left his followers speechless or dumbfounded by the way he conducted his ministry. Jesus didn't come to win a political campaign or set an agenda for maintaining an effective healthcare or healing ministry. Jesus came so that we might "have life, and have it abundantly" (John 10:10). Abundant life does not mean a life full of certainty or truth or health; it means that in the fullness of time, Jesus lived and died so that we might have fullness of life in our time.

We must be willing to admit that the message of Jesus can be messy and difficult. I recently attended a campus ministry event where we read Jesus' words in Matthew's Gospel about putting a millstone around your neck and throwing yourself in the depth of the sea rather than causing another person to stumble (Matt 18:6). We grappled with the text for a while and wondered if Jesus meant what he said. While we didn't come to any concrete conclusions on the pros or cons of millstones around necks, this was precisely the kind of conversation millennials need to have.

When we're *certain* about the interpretation of Scripture or *certain* about what Jesus meant, we start down a slippery slope toward bibliolatry. Instead, we should wrestle with the text, question the text, even doubt the text to gain a deeper understanding of what Jesus might have meant by what he said and did. We live some 2,000 years after the resurrection, so we must interpret and learn together as people who approach the text with healthy expectations and ideas for what we are to receive. If we go looking for concrete answers, we either lie to ourselves or are sorely disappointed. If we go to the text looking for an encounter with a first-century Messiah who challenges our comforts and comforts our challenges, we might find something unique in the Bible. We might find ourselves face to face with a Christ who seeks to invigorate the text with grace and with resurrection.

An Encounter on the Road to Emmaus

The first sermon I preached at the first church I officially served as a staff member was about the road to Emmaus. To this day I remember the sermon title, "Is This More than Just Heartburn?" In the Scripture, the disciples of Jesus suddenly realize over dinner that Jesus had been walking alongside them on the road to Emmaus. They said to one another, "Were not our hearts burning within us while he was talking to us on the road, while he was opening the scriptures to us?" (Luke 24:32).

To quote Ram Dass, "We're all just walking each other home." We're all walking on the road to Emmaus. Jesus saddles up beside us and offers us the grace and strength to follow him. We may not recognize him at first, especially if we are used to a Eurocentric vision of who Jesus was and is, but at the breaking of the bread—at a sacred moment of clarity—we realize that our hearts were burning within us all along. We have known Jesus because he has known us. Since before the dawn of time, Jesus knew that our lives would be tangled up with his life. So we are left as faithful church people to be willing to share with others our encounters and entanglements with Jesus.

If we want to talk about Jesus effectively to a millennial audience, then we must first try to grasp our own entanglement with Jesus. Where did Jesus meet you? Was your experience like Timothy's with the faith of those who raised him? Was it like Paul's on the road to Damascus? Was it like that of the disciples on the road to Emmaus who didn't "get it" until later? Whatever the case, as we better understand the risen and living Christ, we enable others to do the same. By our own encounter, we encourage others to touch, taste, and see that the Lord is good.

Why Are You Afraid?

My spiritual formation group at Duke Divinity School, a group of mostly millennials, gathers every Tuesday morning to discuss our week, where we have seen God and where God has been absent. One morning our spiritual formation director gave us a list of questions that Jesus asked his disciples and other people during his ministry. The first question on the list she gave us jumped off the page. It comes from Matthew 8:26, "Why are you afraid?" The context of Jesus' question is a great, life-threatening storm that comes up while he and the disciples are at sea. As with most of their experiences in the Gospel narrative, the disciples don't get it. The God of angel armies is in the boat with them, so rightfully Jesus asks them why they are afraid. If the God who formed the earth out of primordial waters is in the boat with you, then you have no reason to fear.

I think Jesus' question "Why are you afraid?" echoes down through the centuries to our time and social location. Many of us have never known life in a post-Christian society, but all signs seem to be pointing to it. If we do, in fact, live in a post-Christian society, I still think Jesus asks the question, "Why are you afraid?" Because in reality, our ministry in this society might look a little more like Jesus' ministry. In reality, our time in this society might be exactly what the church needs. I am confident that, ultimately, this is where Jesus is. Just as Jesus after his resurrection told his disciples to go to Galilee and expect him there, we are told to work, to cultivate, to mend fences in this post-Christian society, and we are told to go into our future to meet Jesus there.

The problem of religious "nones" is that we've done this to ourselves. We've made our crumbling institution a god instead of worshiping the God who redeems the institution. Institutions certainly have value; this book is a testament to that. But everything within the institution must be examined and articulated in a way that is fruitful for a millennial mindset, or it must be trimmed for the sake of authentic discipline to the way of following Jesus.

The Messianic Promise

The story goes that a failing monastery had tried everything to keep its doors open. One day, in frustration, the abbot went to meet with the rabbi who lived on the edge of town and usually kept to himself. As they met, the abbot articulated his anxiety over the closing of the monastery, but the rabbi assured him the monastery would not close. "The Messiah is in your midst," the rabbi said. As the statement resonated with him, the abbot rushed back to the monastery to tell his brothers that the Messiah, the one meant to save humanity, was in their midst. Then something remarkable happened. They started treating each other like they would treat the Messiah. Their language toward each other, the way they conducted themselves, and everything else that could possibly change did so for the better because the Messiah was in their midst. Numbers of people started to come and see this reborn monastery, and young men committed their lives to the order because of the way they treated one another.

The story of the monastery encapsulates the point of this chapter. If we're going to start appealing to millennials, then we'll have to act like a church that knows and has seen Jesus. We must be a church that has been brought to the point of death and found resurrection there. We must be a church that has been led to a cross and found Jesus on it. For there, and there only, will our crumbling institutions be reshaped for the twenty-first century.

Notes

1. Fred Kaan, "We Meet You O Christ," Hope Publishing Company, 1968.

2. Michael Lipka, "A Closer Look at America's Rapidly Growing Religious 'Nones'" Pew Research Center, 13 May 2015, http://www.pewresearch.org/fact-tank/2015/05/13/a-closer-look-at-americas-rapidly-growing-religious-nones/.

3. Sam Wells, "The Word We Don't Mention," *Faith & Leadership*, 14 May 2009, https://www.faithandleadership.com/sermons/the-word-we-don't-mention? (accessed 20 October 2016).

Chapter 7

REFLECTIONS FROM THE STAINED GLASS

with Morgan Bell

I feel most called to ministry in those raw, intimate moments—those times when ministers are invited into peoples' lives to speak the gospel words of hope; to hold them up in prayer; to bring them the sacraments. —Morgan Bell

I have never met Morgan Bell in person, but I'm confident that when we finally do meet, it will be like two old friends have run into each other. Morgan is from Canada and currently pursuing ministry within the United Church of Canada. This chapter provides a unique perspective, especially for those of us in the United States.

Canada is not as religiously affiliated as the United States, and we can learn something from our neighbors to the north as church attendance declines here in the States. We can learn that authentic worship can be found in small groups of committed people who are driven for the building of God's kingdom on earth. Take heart, people of God: God is not done with us yet.

Morgan Bell is a student at Trent University in Peterborough, Ontario, and is studying French literature. He is a candidate for ordered (ordained) ministry in the United Church of Canada.

Rob Lee: Tell me how you were called to the ministry.

Morgan Bell: People often ask me when I knew that I wanted to be a minister. I usually say that I knew in about grade 11, and I came to terms with that calling in my second year of university. Being from a small, rural congregation, I was often given the opportunity to do pulpit supply, and I have been a longtime organist at our church. Church was a large part of my life growing up, even if it wasn't part of my family life.

In university, I was a residence adviser and I often noted that this wasn't just "peer counseling" or "advising"; it was pastoral care. I started to see myself connecting my faith with my work in a way I hadn't experienced before.

I started to realize that many things I loved to do and that I was good at aligned tightly to a minister's skill set. I love to preach, I love writing prayers, I love talking and working with people, and I don't even hate church board meetings. But you see, these are the things I love about ministry. They aren't necessarily why I feel called to ministry.

I feel most called to ministry in those raw, intimate moments—those times when ministers are invited into peoples' lives to speak the gospel words of hope; to hold them up in prayer; to bring them the sacraments. After being asked to preside at a handful of funerals and after counseling folks in the depths of depression or on the verge of dangerous self-harm, I began to realize that this was a life to which I was called. So, after much prayer and consternation, I said it out loud: "I think God is calling me to be a minister."

And it felt right.

Why buy stock in a dying organization? That is to say, why are you pursuing a calling that many millennials and people your age have given up?

There are many examples in history when the church, for various reasons, should have died. There is no logical reason that the church has institutionally survived for as long as it has. I won't go into that history here, as a large amount of literature has been written chronicling that phenomenon.

But here's the thing: the church didn't die. Granted, it has changed, morphed, and adapted, but the church didn't die. The gospel continues to be lived out by billions of faithful men and women across the globe, and the church is in fact growing in the global south. I don't view myself as "buying stock in a dying organization." A friend once asked me about my vocation, "Would you marry a woman with stage IV cancer?" A penetrating question indeed. But the more I thought about it, the more I realized that it wasn't a fair question. The church has chance for recovery. The church can carry on, and I have faith that it will. We have work to do. Yet ultimately the church isn't ours to administer and manage, is it? To paraphrase Céline Dion, "[The church] will go on"!

But let us say it doesn't. Let us imagine that the church does die. What will we do? Where will we go? How will we be Christians in community?

The answer is simple: we are a people who profess a risen Lord. We believe that where there is death, there is also resurrection. Life is found in the darkest places. We can worry about the future and make plans for it, but ultimately we don't despair. We trust that, though we have control over certain elements of our organizations and structures, God is ultimately in control. And every time we celebrate the sacraments, welcome new members, or help others in times of raw need, we are reminded that God is not done with us yet.

How has your calling affected your relationships, friendships, and family dynamics? Are they concerned you're interested in a precarious ministry? What is your response to them?

Entering ministry in this day and age is a scary prospect. Who knows where the church will be in ten, twenty, forty years? I know of ministers who burn out after five to ten years. Many must turn to a bi-vocational approach simply to make ends meet. Debt-riddled churches are widespread. Things look grim.

My immediate family knows that. We were never a churchgoing family; my aunt took me to church when I was a child. I do not think for one moment that my family doesn't support me, but they voice their concerns about the sustainability of such a "job." Will I even have one near the end of my career? It's a tough question.

Friends are almost all onboard. My extended family, after hearing me officiate at a funeral, all expressed their support. What I find interesting is that these are non-church folk. They may have grown up in the church, but they all fell away as responsibilities and obligations stacked up.

To the ones who often express doubts or concerns about my vocation, I remind them that they are envisioning me in a stereotypical ministry context: small, rural church; handful of old ladies who make up the congregation; boring service; ham-and-salad suppers—the works.

And I'm not suggesting that I won't end up ministering in such a context. But I am quick to remind them that there are other expressions of doing church. We focus on the death and debt, but there are countless examples of congregations who are doing well, and that is a sign of hope.

Yes, the church will continue to decline. Churches will close. It will be tough. But part of the United Church of Canada's supplementary statement of faith, "A New Creed," defiantly states,

> In life, in death, in life-beyond-death,
> God is with us.
> We are not alone.

God is still speaking. We need only faithfully listen and follow.

Where have you seen God in the millennial generation?

Much has been written about the "spiritual-but-not-religious" (SBNR) folks and the infamous "nones." These are folks with no real connection to any one religious tradition. However, it is often noted that they experience sacred moments more often than religious folks in the decades preceding our generation.

When I speak to friends who identify as SBNR or a "none," I'm often blown away that they are constantly seeking a sacred experience or a spiritual encounter, though they may not use that language. These are folks who are searching for an authentic spirituality that speaks to who they are. They look for a community that is supportive and uplifting.

In his book *A Secular Age*, Charles Taylor observes that trend. Folks are no longer looking for an authoritative spirituality; they are looking for an *authentic* spirituality. I have been to many churches that I believe made this transition from authority to authenticity, and they were full of millennials and young adults.

These churches didn't abandon the Gospels or their doctrines, or swap out the Eucharist for a time of yoga or coffee hour. They steeped themselves so fully in the life and work of Jesus Christ that their community was deeply infused with a burning desire to live in response to God's redeeming, regenerating love. They let their theology animate their faith. They let their worship guide their governance. They kept the faith authentically and witnessed the gospel in all they did together. And folks are drawn to them.

A craving for God doesn't just disappear because the church is losing influence. One doesn't stop being hungry when there isn't food in the house. What do you do? You find your food elsewhere. I believe that we're seeing folks turn to other channels and mediums to connect with the Sacred. The millennial generation yearns for God, whether we express it like that or not.

What gives you the most hope about the church?

You don't have to look far to find hope. "Hope" isn't just a word that we find in our Scriptures and profess in our liturgies. Our churches need to reflect the hope that is found in Jesus and live into that hope. R. C. Sproul wrote, "Hope is called the anchor of the soul, because it gives stability to the Christian life. But hope is not simply a 'wish' (I wish that such-and-such would take place); rather, it is that which latches on to the certainty of the promises of the future that God has made."

Each time we share in the bread and the wine, I see and partake in hope. Each time someone enters the church for worship, I see hope. Each time we feed or help someone who is struggling under a burden, I see hope. In times of deep prayer, corporate or otherwise, we see and respond to that hope. Our hope is alive.

Just because our finances are tight or because our buildings and parishioners are old or because a life of faith isn't popular does not mean we do not live out Christ's mission in our world: a mission of faith, hope, and love. My greatest hope in the church is, and must be, Jesus Christ; for in him we find our mission, our guide, and our redemption.

Why stay? Why now? Why be a part of this movement that is slowing down?

There's a saying often attributed to Mahatma Gandhi: Be the change you wish to see in the world. I think I need to answer God's call because I have gifts that the church needs. I think we all do.

To be sure, I'm not saying that I'm going to single-handedly save the church or inspire revitalization within the denomination or even pastor a growing congregation. No. That's larger than one person.

However, I do believe that I can bring Christian witness to a liberal denomination that often shies away from personal testimony or even from strong theological stances. I believe I can espouse an orthodox theology and liberal-progressive beliefs—two concepts often seen to be at odds. I think that I can speak a word of hope that, in concert with all the other voices singing of God's love, can ignite the world. I have faith and I have the means to live out that faith, if I only answer the call.

A line in the gospel song "Oh, Happy Day!" proclaims that "He taught me how to live rejoicing!" We have a faith that demands hard work, often sacrifice. But to follow Jesus Christ is to live life to the fullest: to love, to laugh, to suffer, to live with ardor and a compassion that knows no bounds. How can you turn away from that?

What are your hopes for the future of the institutional church?

I am often quite taken with places such as the Community of Taizé or Iona Abbey. These are communities that practice ancient forms of worship and, by all accounts, have a fairly orthodox theology. Coming from a progressive denomination that sometimes falls into the trap of thinking that we need a more progressive (in my opinion, borderline watered-down) theology in order to "attract" millennials, I find it refreshing that communities such as Taizé or Iona do the exact opposite.

They follow the Liturgy of the Hours. They have daily Eucharist. They use chant to evoke powerful, sacred experiences. They commit their lives to prayer and to living out the Gospels in a drastic way.

And we millennials love it. People travel from all over the world to have a glimpse at a life fully immersed in Jesus Christ, and then they take that renewed spirituality with them.

My hope for the institutional church is that we realize that our mission is not to be "relevant" or "cool." If I wanted coffee hour, I would go to a coffee shop. If I wanted a social justice club, I'd join one. If I wanted a feel-good theology, I would look to the self-help section at my local bookstore.

But I don't.

I look for a community that is brought together by a common faith. I crave a church that acts on that faith of justice, resurrection, redemption, and unconditional love. I don't want a watered-down gospel; I want to be challenged by Jesus' vision for an upside-down kingdom of God where the weak are strong and none are afraid. Such a church not only facilitates the transformation of its members but also works to transform the world. My hope for the church is that we claim the identity we are given as children of God and that we live authentically in response to that extraordinary love.

REFLECTION QUESTIONS

• Morgan is a part of the United Church of Canada; Canada is a largely post-Christian society. How might Christians in the United States learn to operate in a culture headed to look similar to Canada's?

• Morgan talks about the gifts he brings to the church. What gifts do you offer to bring to the institutional church?

• Morgan talks about the "raw, intimate moments of ministry." Where and when have you experienced those moments in your own life?

Chapter 8

WHY JOIN A CHURCH NOW?

Reshaping Church Membership in a Millennial Mindset

Saints cannot exist without a community as they require, like all of us, nurturance by a people who, while often unfaithful, preserve the habits necessary to learn the story of God. —Stanley Hauerwas[1]

When I drive through rural North Carolina, it's easy for me to guess a church's theology based on its outward appearance. We've unfortunately placed ourselves in tiny boxes that define who we are. In a world where individual spirituality is taking over the norms of what religion laid claim to for centuries, it's alarming to talk about church. We've forsaken talking about the institutional church because it doesn't fit into our nice, neat realities where spirituality will sustain us.

Don't get me wrong; spirituality is an incredible resource for the faithful. Some of the early church fathers and mothers were mystics who sustained themselves on spirituality, but they also had a deep and abiding affection for the church universal. In a world where "spiritual but not religious" is taking over, what good can the church do for the millennial generation who would prefer to spend their Sundays shopping or catching up on sleep?

The catch with spirituality without religion is that it does not offer intentional community, and faith without community isn't effective. I think of my own life: Was I not formed and shaped by church members who loved me at my baptism and confirmation? Was I not challenged by pastors who saw good in me in spite of what I saw in myself? Such significant instances in the life of this millennial have taken place in community. They would not have been possible without community!

Community around God's resurrecting power is what religion offers. We are invited into the divine dance that has been going on well before we were born. Through corporate worship, through acts of caring ministry, and through the realities of shared communal life, we see the beauty that community can offer millennials if we are just willing to accept it.

How does the church offer community to millennials? In this chapter, I use the United Methodist version of membership vows as an example. What might millennials gain from this version of community? When joining the United Methodist Church, people are asked, "As members of this congregation, will you faithfully participate in its ministries by your prayers, your presence, your gifts, your service, and your witness?"[2] This is a good question to ponder, and each element has meaning.

Prayers

I will cover more about corporate worship in chapter 10 (Reforming Worship for a Millennial Generation), but for the sake of this chapter I want to focus on corporate prayer as a means of forming community. Many of us have been uplifted, comforted, and affirmed by communal prayer. We have joined together as sinners with a past and saints with a future in prayer for one another and with one another. Why would the church not want to offer that to my generation as a hallmark of community? I think one of the most important tenets of community is praying for and with each other in times of joy and times of trial.

This can be hard. We spend our lives in a millennial mindset of go-go-go and find ourselves scraping time for prayer only at Sunday worship—if we even make that time a time of prayer. What if thought of prayer like a conversation that begins with our waking and ends with our sleeping?

At Duke University, one of my assignments was to create a journal of prayer and theological reflections surrounding Psalm 73. At first I thought this was busywork, but as I was forced into carving out part of my day for prayer and reflection on the songbook of the Bible, I found myself enlivened and filled with hope. And the beauty of prayer is this: you don't have to convince someone to attend church every Sunday to let him or her know you are praying. I am convinced that even ardent atheists can be humbled to know that people are lifting them up in their hearts and thoughts to a Being higher than both groups, regardless if one of them believes or not.

During my time serving a church in a pastoral role, one of the frustrations communicated to me by my generation was that when people say they're praying for you, many millennials wonder if they actually mean it. I too, have often been guilty of saying I would pray for someone and then, in the busyness of life, forgetting the importance of fulfilling my commitments to pray in beloved community for that person.

My answer to this is simple: mean what you say. If you're going to say that you're praying for someone, do it. Even if that means offering a prayer then and there, be authentic when you say you're going to pray for someone. The hope of prayer is that we will have an encounter with God, and in that encounter we might be changed.

Millennials need to join in prayer and be lifted in prayer. Through this prayerful mindset, we see the beauty of community, of communal and corporate prayer, and of joining our voices with angels, archangels, and all the company of heaven, praising and petitioning the Creator of us all.

Presence

My high school English teacher Wanda McConnell taught me two things that I remember to this day: always commit pen to paper, and 95 percent of life is showing up. She told this to a young high school boy who had trouble showing up to class, a millennial who wasn't ready to commit pen to paper. And those words ring true for me still. Part of community is being present.

My friend Kelli once told me that we have to take part in certain things in this life to show that we are alive. Being present in community means seeing the joys of life and the terrible, incomprehensible sorrows of life. Millennials could use presence right about now. In a post 9/11 world where media and social media compress and abbreviate everything around us, sometimes the real presence of a human body is overlooked. People are meeting each other, dating, and conversing online and through social media. We have forgotten the beauty of presence.

When millennials and the church are present with one another, we see the beauty of shared experience and learn that can re-create and reform relationships that were lost by time. There is intrinsic beauty in knowing that I have a church family who will be present with me as I walk this road of life. And while millennials may not value church as much, they certainly value community and presence. In this mindset, the church must reshape its understanding of community to be present with and in the lives of millennials. This means reaching out in modes and methods familiar to millennials. This means creating space and time for millennials to be present with those of different generations and social locations.

By being present with and for people of different generations, we are committing ourselves to the resurrecting work of the church. We are reminding ourselves that there are those who have come before us and those who will come after us. Presence is so much more than being around people; it is being *with* people. With them in their sorrow and in their joy, in their pain and in their dancing. I have a friend who was going through some medical issues, and I asked him how I could be present with him in his suffering. He said he wished more people would adapt that mindset. We are so busy trying to fix everything that we forget the simple presence of a hug or a silent moment with another person. We use what we have to be a present reality for someone. We are the presence of Christ in some instances, and that is something no generation (millennials included) should take lightly.

Gifts

Ask a millennial to give to the church, and it may be the church's death sentence. My generation is afraid to give to any institution known for mishandling and mistreating financial resources entrusted to it. The church has not always been good with money, but neither have millennials. In a world where student debt is crippling the millennial generation for what may be their entire lives, the church is going to have to think through what it means to give faithfully to its mission.

When I served First Baptist Church, West Jefferson, we learned something that I think could benefit the wider church. Yes, we could preach the dreary stewardship sermon in which we beg for the sake of the widow's mite or riches gaining rust, but what people really want to hear is what the church would do with the money if we were lucky enough to get it. During worship, we invited people, millennial and gen-X and baby boomer alike, to tell the story of the church. We heard the sacred story of First Baptist Church, and we heard why our ministry matters.

My senior minister was onto something. He pointed out to me that, when asked to support the building of a new parking lot, the boomer generation replied, "How much would the project cost?" and "Can we make it happen?" Nowadays, if the church wants to build a parking lot, the millennial generation asks, "Why do we need this?" and "What would be gained by building this parking lot?" These shifts in the attitudes of generations paint a reality in the church that must be addressed. The reality is this: we don't have the resources we once had, so how are we going to operate?

The church as a leaner organization doesn't always spell demise. Going back to my time at First Baptist, instead of hiring full time staff, we relied heavily on part-time ministry professionals who created a space for more ministry to happen. We reshaped our staff for the sake of the mission of the church. Millennials don't want to work in heavily organized structures; they want people who are invested in every way. This means we must put our money where our mouth is across the board. We are commanded to give to the work and ministry of the church through our tithes and offerings. In doing so, we set an example for our generations and for our churches to be faithful stewards of the things entrusted to us.

I will be the first to admit that giving in any generation is hard. Especially in the current economic climate, it is hard to find faithful and fruitful givers to the church. And if you do find a giver who is faithful and fruitful, sustaining that level of giving for a lifetime (as church members were able to in years past) is increasingly hard.

In summary, giving is one of the hardest parts of being a member of the church. But the church must reimagine what it means to give: giving is based not on the principle that the church needs the money to survive but on the principle that people *need* to give to survive. We are giving creatures, and we are meant to share what we have. In this mindset, we give because we need to give, not because the church needs us to. Churches must be faithful stewards of said giving, but if you're in such a faithful church, more often than not you will see the fruits of your giving.

Service

In a lecture one day, Bishop Will Willimon told us about a church that invited young adult millennials to come on a Friday evening and meet some of the church's friends. The young people arrived and found that they were befriending and working with the homeless, and those young people served them through interacting with their stories.

What does service look like for millennials? It takes shape in the groundwork that creates and restores relationships with people. It is work that builds and sustains community. Through our service, we see the realities and complexities of our time in tangible ways. We see the vast wealth disparity in this country, we see the failings of the church to make a difference, and we see the racial divide that is only getting wider and deeper. It is in this context that the church can truly work.

Faith without works is dead (Jas 2:17). We are charged to serve those around us. But twenty-first-century American millennials have a different idea of service than what God asks of us. We want benefit from our service. We want to pursue the service of others for the sake of our own gratification and, dare I say, sanctification. But we must shift this mindset to create an economy of service so that we serve not only the less fortunate but also our spouses, our friends, our family, and those around us whom we consider equal. We must adopt an attitude of service that seeks to create a new reality in which God is working to bring about God's kingdom in every single person we encounter.

We are ultimately sanctified through our service because it enlivens our faith. But seeking service simply to get the "check-plus" by our name to enter into God's eternal kingdom is a pitiful excuse for service. We are called to serve in the name of Jesus for the sake of the gospel. We are called to be churches that serve millennials and to be millennials who serve the church. We must create an environment of service that entrusts our works to God's abiding grace. When we do this, we will see that millennials will invest in it. Millennials want to be a part of something that seeks to create life for others.

At Duke, I have a friend who insists on serving me dinner on occasion. I don't know if she realizes the task she is undertaking since I am such a picky eater, but nonetheless she seeks to create a palatable meal for me. At first I was hesitant to let her do this, because frankly I would rather be the person who serves by buying a meal. But as I have learned to accept her service and kindness, I have been opened to a new realm of grace. For God is in our service. God is in our encounters with one another. At this juncture, God is found. The Spirit sends us into the world to serve and be agents of service. But the Spirit also encourages us to be recipients of service.

Witness

When the 2008 General Conference of the United Methodist Church changed the liturgy of the membership covenant to add "Witness" to the vows, most Methodists barely batted an eye. The hymnal and liturgy didn't change unless the pastor slipped it in under his or her breath when someone was joining the church. For some, witnessing sounds too evangelical for their progressive minds, and for others, it seems too little too late.

But what does witnessing have to do with our personal works of faith as members of a church? More important, how do we engage in witnessing in a millennial world? To answer the first question, we must accept that our faith is to be proclaimed in ways that lead people to a greater understanding of the grace offered to them in their baptism. It is our holy honor to have those sacred stories intricately woven into our lives, but it is even more important to share those stories with those around us.

Think about it this way: the 2012 movie *Silver Linings Playbook* chronicles the journey of someone reentering society after being released from a behavioral health facility. The story is woven in a way that the man finds sanity and love in the most unlikely place. In the climactic scene, the protagonist's father proclaims, "You have to pay attention to signs. When life reaches out with a moment like this, it's a sin if you don't reach back . . . I'm telling you."[3]

That movie was onto something: we must pay attention to the signs of our time. We are called to be stewards of sacred stories of faith. The gospel will not share itself! The beauty in all of this is that the script has been written, and we are simply told to share the story in a way that reflects our understanding of our tradition and experience.

I am aware that witnessing may not be the most "fashionable" term for some church circles. But we're going to have to be missional again for the sake of millennials. The reality is that they need to hear a good word from the church. They need to hear why Jesus is Lord of the church, and they need to hear how that has affected our lives and beings. When we witness to them, we are retelling the stories to ourselves, reminding us that even the stories we've known forever can take on new meaning in the light of God's glory and grace.

Reshaping Church Membership

Though I have focused on the membership vows of the United Methodist Church, many other denominations ask similar questions of their members. My goal was to show that the reality of our time and place is that membership matters. We are formed, shaped, and called by community. Spirituality is nice and has merits, but it certainly has limits. How do we reshape and reform the understanding of membership? We do so by taking our membership vows seriously.

In her book *Searching for Sunday*, Rachel Held Evans puts it this way:

> In my struggle to find church, I've often felt that if I could just find the right denomination or the right congregation, if I could just become the right person or believe the right things, then my search would be over at last. But right's got nothing to do with it. Waiting around for right will leave you waiting around forever. The church is God saying: "I'm throwing a banquet, and all these mismatched, messed-up people are invited. Here, have some wine."[4]

Our sure and certain hope is that we are formed in community. We are shaped by the community that surrounds us. We are offered the finest bread, wine, and water for the sake of community to share with one another. It is perfect in its imperfection.

When I was growing up at Broad Street United Methodist Church, we'd have an infant baptism for a grandson, niece, or friend of a member at Broad Street. While it was a valuable moment in the life of that child, I remember my mom leaving in frustration after most of those services. I eventually found out why. Mom took seriously the claim the church makes when it says it will nurture and raise each child in the community of faith. Often, the church was baptizing babies we might never see again. While I'm not debating the efficacy of the baptism, if we take the vows we make in church as seriously as our marriage vows, church might look a little different.

In the end, when people of any generation take membership vows, they should lead by example. They should continue the good work that was started in them at baptism and keep it going until the fruition of God's plan for their lives is made clear on the last day. Through prayers, presence, gifts, service, and witness, we see that community is built over time. While some may consider millennials impatient, these young people do see the beauty in investment. Churches should invite this generation to invest where the beauty of tradition meets the innovation of the twenty-first century: community. Through shared experience and community-building activities, the church has the potential to reclaim this generation for the good of the church and the sake of the gospel.

The next time I'm driving through North Carolina and looking at churches, it is my hope that I'll be pleasantly surprised by innovative churches that are taking membership seriously. Maybe I'll see churches that have changed their memberships to focus more on community instead of homogeneity or social location. Maybe I'll see more places where everyone is welcome and diversities are celebrated through prayers, presence, gifts, service, and witness. This is my hope. Let's make it happen.

Notes

1. Stanley Hauerwas, "The Gesture of a Truthful Story," available at http://people.duke.edu/~kns15/Gesture.pdf (accessed 20 October 2016).

2. The Baptismal Covenant I" in The United Methodist Hymnal (Nashville: The United Methodist Publishing House, 1989) 38.

3. *Silver Linings Playbook*, dir. David O. Russell, The Weinstein Company and Mirage Enterprises, 2012.

4. Rachel Held Evans, *Searching for Sunday: Loving, Leaving, and Finding the Church* (Nashville: Thomas Nelson, 2015).

Chapter 9

REFLECTIONS FROM THE STAINED GLASS

with The Reverend Sara E. Smith

As a woman of the millennial generation who is an ordained minister, I feel that it is a great part of my calling to help be a plank in the bridge that is being formed between the institutional church of the past generations and the church of the current and future generations.
—*Sara Smith*

I first encountered Sara Smith at First Baptist Church in West Jefferson, North Carolina. I had just started my job and was ready to make a difference in the world. When I met her, she was preparing to begin her studies at Wake Forest Divinity School. I've had the privilege of participating in her ordination and have come to count her as wise counsel in my life. Sara has a unique story of finding her vocational call and identity in a place of confusion that gave way to a beautiful reality of ministry.

As you read the next few pages, I challenge you to place yourself within her story. Find the beauty of being called without knowing how to express that fully until God comes in and gives you a fresh anointing of God's sufficient grace.

The Reverend Sara Smith is a graduate of North Carolina State University and Wake Forest Divinity School. She is a chaplain resident at Wake Forest Baptist Medical Center in Winston-Salem, North Carolina.

Rob Lee: Tell me how you were called to the ministry.

Sara Smith: My journey to answering the call to be a chaplain was one filled with many detours. Growing up, I was always drawn to church and to religion. However, I never saw church or religion as a place where I personally could propel forward as a career. When entering college, I put myself on the path to working in the medical field. I did, and still do, have a great passion for medicine and the advancements that are taking place in the field. But it was in college that I felt an odd pulling toward something more. I continued to be involved in church activities and religious thought, and even invested four consecutive summers working for Passport, Inc.

My passion and love for ministry grew with each passing year until I finally could deny it no longer. I was in a place of confusion. How was I to move forward after graduating with a degree in cellular and molecular biology and somehow create a ministry career? It took a lot of thoughtful meditation and prayer, as well as many long discussions with my friends, family, mentors, and pastor, before the thought of pursuing chaplain ministry formed in my being. When the feeling finally struck, there was no way of denying it. Chaplaincy ministry was what I was meant to do with my life in the current moment. Throughout divinity school, my studies revolved around that goal, and my life was forever changed. My passions of medicine and ministry were finally reconciled to one another in a way that created good in the world of people around me who searched for joy and comfort on a minute-by-minute basis.

Why buy stock in a dying organization? That is to say, why are you pursuing a calling that many millennials have given up?

In my opinion, I do not think people of my generation have given up on religion. Instead, I think religion has not grown to meet the people of my generation. The world and everything in it is in a state of constant flux and evolution. Religion is not shielded from this type of change. However, religion can sometimes be resistant to types of generational changes. As a generation that survives on innovation and is always hoping for "the next new idea," religion can sometimes be seen as a thing of the past. That is exactly why I hold tightly to and buy stock in a dying organization such as the church and chaplaincy. As a woman of the millennial generation who is an ordained minister, I feel that it is a great part of my calling to help be a plank in the bridge that is being formed between the institutional church of the past generations and the church of the current and future generations.

Being a voice of reason and change will hopefully help bring the church into the viewpoint of the current generation as an institution that is still very much alive and well. Also, I think chaplaincy is something that people will always need in some shape or form. We have all been born into this world. The reality of the matter is that we will all at some point encounter death, and eventually die ourselves. As a called chaplain in this current generation, it is my job to help those in the face of death or sadness or grief name their emotions and work through them in a way that is sensitive to their spiritual (or nonspiritual) needs.

How has your calling affected your relationships, friendships, and family dynamics? Are they concerned that you're interested in a precarious ministry? What is your response to them?

The changes in my relationships since answering the call to ministry have happened in small bits over the course of the past few years. At first, my relationships did not seem to change much at all. People still acted the same way around me or towards me. Then little things began to happen. People began either to distance themselves from me when they were talking about certain more "worldly" issues or to be cautious with their words and phrases. Then I began to feel a bit of judgment from others in my inner circle with some of the things I said, books I read, reality TV shows I watched, or music I listened to.

Finally, people began to rely on me for answers to questions about religions or when a prayer needed to be said. It took me a little while to register these changes, and then a while longer to come to terms with the fact that these changes were just part of the process of answering a call to public ministry. I decided that people were going to have to get used to me being a minister and also being female, younger, shorter, a fan of country music, a follower of the *Real Housewives* and *The Bachelor* TV shows, and someone who does not always have the answers to difficult questions.

As far as being called into chaplaincy, I think my relationships with others have been strangely strengthened. To be a chaplain, you must be okay with dealing with the messy parts of life. You also must be open, honest, and willing to help carry the burdens of those around you. Because of this, family and friends have become more open around me with their personal struggles. It has allowed me not only to flex my muscles as a minister who is pursuing a vocation in chaplaincy but also to grow closer with those that I hold near and dear to my heart.

Where have you seen God in the millennial generation?

In my opinion, God is a relational God. While Jesus Christ was on this earth, he demonstrated ways in which the hands and feet of God could be actively lived out. And while, yes, the millennial generation may not have a strong physical presence inside many church walls, they have a strong physical and spiritual presence in the greater communities and nations of the world. I feel that this generation is the greatest extension of the hands and feet of Christ. They are sitting and having meals with the marginalized. They are feeding the masses. They are traveling great distances in order to build relationships. They are using their words and their intelligence to oppose systematic oppression and wrong in their communities. They are showing love where sometimes love has never been shown before. If these things are not of God, then I am not sure what would be.

What gives you the most hope about the church?

What gives me the most hope about the church is that walls are no longer required for worship and healing to take place. Nonconventional forms of church and worship are becoming more common in this generation. This gives me hope because sometimes with walls come boxes and stigmas and conformity. And while it may be a goal for mainstream churches to move past these, for now in this generation hope can be found in coffee shops and community gardens, in prayer circles and at hospital bedsides. Hope can be found in almost any place. All that needs to be present is a little faith and a whole lot of love.

Why stay? Why now? Why be a part of this movement that is slowing down?

Why not stay? Why not fight for this thing called church? Why not be a living and breathing example of love and radical hospitality to the world? I think a movement that is slowing down needs ministers who are willing to take chances and be different. It needs people who are willing to try new things but also hold tight to the traditions that created the church. It needs a fresh set of eyes with new ideas and creativity that can bring light to a dimming flame. The time has not passed for the church. The time for the church is right now. That is why I am staying. The church needs us. The church is begging for us. The church is ready for us.

What are your hopes for the future of the institutional church?

I have three goals for the institutional church. The first goal is *inclusion*. This generation is fighting a hard battle for rights of freedom and inclusion for all people. Church is an institution that needs to answer to this call now more than ever. In order for the church to move forward and continue to grow and strengthen, it must be open and welcoming to all people, no matter the circumstances. Outstretched hands of love and welcome may be small, but like a mustard seed they can grow into something much larger than themselves and, in the end, move mountains with faith.

The second goal is *innovation*. The institutional church holds tightly to its traditions. I believe that those traditions can still be kept, but they can be conceptualized in new ways that are conducive to the current and future generations. The sacraments can become revitalized, worship can be reimagined, and community can be transformed. It is possible. Tradition and innovation can live together in harmony. It just takes a little dose of creativity and imagination.

The final goal is *intentionality*. With inclusion and innovation comes intentionality. Sometimes worship in the institutional church can seem like a time when people just go through the motions. I believe that when we are intentional about every word that is said, or every motion or action that is presented, church and worship can be turned into a time where God and the world come face to face. With intentionality, the millennial generation will be able to remain focused on their faith and not on their next social media update.

REFLECTION QUESTIONS

- What part of Sara's story struck you as something that could be part of your own story? How does her story differ from yours?

- Sara lists three goals for the institutional church. What might you add to that list?

- What from Sara's story gives you hope?

Chapter 10

REFORMING WORSHIP FOR A MILLENNIAL GENERATION

So has the church in liturgy and song, in faith and love, through centuries of wrong, borne witness to the truth in every tongue, Alleluia!
—Fred Pratt Green[1]

How Worship and Liturgy Changed My Life

Between my junior and senior years of high school, I had a summer like none other. While some high schoolers were heavily into sports camps or band camps, I decided to go to a camp for theologians. The Duke Youth Academy changed my life. Dr. Fred Edie heads the program for high school students at Duke Divinity School, and in *Book, Bath, Table, Time*, he writes,

> We tend to ask, "How can we make worship more appealing to our youth?" rather than, "How can we ensure that youth will encounter the fullness of the presence of the living God in worship?" One question is framed by the market, the other by the theological tradition. One thinks first about the need of young consumers and how to produce experiences to satisfy those needs. The other recognizes God's presence is the gift (freely and graciously given, not for sale, no marketing required) of the incarnation mediated through book, bath, table, and time. One question implicitly supports a world ordered around consumption; the second question explicitly renounces it and instead names and enacts a reign of grace, justice, and peace.[2]

The Duke Youth Academy is formational—a place where community life is intrinsically linked with worshiping life. Throughout the model of the program, worship is central. For the time the students attend the program, they are taught how to worship deeper and given the opportunity to lead in meaningful and authentic worship.

Worship changed my life and continues to change my life. It is the source of my greatest joy in the church, for in worship we are bound together and catch glimpses of the kingdom of God. Though I had experienced that before coming to the Duke Youth Academy, the academy solidified the fact that the worshiping life is the life for me. But deeper than that, the worshiping life is a life that needs to be shared.

Community-driven Worship

In previous chapters, I have discussed the millennial generation's intrinsic need for community. For those needs to be met, there must be shared practice and work that the people do together for the betterment of themselves and the community of which they are a part. This buy-in creates cohesion.

"Liturgy" literally means the work of the people. The act of worship and sacrament performed by the church through the ages is the central aspect of Christian community. However, with the millennials' lack of education in "churchspeak," it's impossible to know if someone has understood the beauty of worship in their time and place. This has to change. If the church wants to lay claim to the millennial generation, it must seek to reframe worship in a way that is appealing and challenging to millennials.

When one thinks of worship in modernity, the worship wars have two main camps: contemporary and traditional styles. These two camps have dominated the conversation for the past twenty years; all the while, millennials are leaving the church. It's time for the debate to stop. Let your yes be yes and your no be no (Matt 5:37). That is, churches should accept their identity as contemporary or traditional and work to make sure that, regardless of style, their worship is acceptable in the eyes of God.

For millennials, the work and worship of the people is about authenticity. My generation sniffs out inauthentic worship and then avoids it. So how do we reframe the blessed sacraments and worship components in an authentic way? The answer has the potential to be complex or simple depending on your context.

The answer to inauthentic worship is the practice of liturgy. The word proclaimed and the celebration of the table and font brings together a broken community. In that light, we see the beauty of authentic worship: broken and flawed people working toward perfection. Millennials appreciate vulnerability and authenticity, and where can the church accomplish both of these acts? Through our worship and through our liturgical actions.

Hymnody for Millennials

Whether a church's style of worship is contemporary or traditional or blended, what we sing and how we sing it is important because music often speaks when words or sermons filled with theological platitudes fail. I say this as a person who loves to preach. I say it with the realization that sometimes my words in sermons will not do the trick for some people.

I first learned this lesson in my undergraduate years at Appalachian State University. I was looking for a class to fill, so I found one in the Music Department that seemed interesting. Little did I know the far-sweeping effects this class would have on my life. The class was titled "Liturgies," and I knew I was in for a treat when organist and professor Dr. Joby Bell walked in. His wit and wisdom is something I will cherish for the rest of my career. I remember him telling me when I interviewed him for my faith column, "Worship is best well rehearsed and well received. We as a species invented worship, and though we invented it, we need to get it right because it's not all about us."

Bell is spot on. Hymnody is important regardless of style. Take for instance a debate the Presbyterian Church U.S.A. had surrounding the worship song "In Christ Alone." When debating what to include in their new hymnal, *Glory to God*, they took a look at this song. The original lyrics go like this: "And on that cross, as Jesus died, the wrath of God was satisfied." The Presbyterian Committee on Congregational Song wanted to change the words from "wrath of God was satisfied" to "love of God was magnified." The original composers of the song's lyrics objected to that change, so the committee opted to drop the song from the hymnbook.

Regardless of what you think about the merits (or lack thereof) of the substitutionary atonement theology presented in that song, you can see the point I'm making. What we sing matters because of what it says about the height, depth, and breadth of our theology. And trust me when I say millennials are paying attention. Music is important to any up-and-coming generation. Music speaks and people listen. So it is best that the music the church puts out or chooses to sing is a loudspeaker of theology and polity.

If the church wants to reclaim the millennial generation, then we must undertake theological thinking as we plan the liturgy and hymnody in our worship services. Countless times I have found myself listening to an anthem or signing a hymn in church and then realizing I have to follow it with my preaching. It can be daunting and difficult, but music done well is imperative for authentic worship.

Preaching to a Millennial Generation

I am a preacher by trade. It is what I was called and created for. The craft of preaching is my favorite thing to do in the church. I'm reminded of Kierkegaard's words:

> Alas, in regard to things spiritual, the foolishness of many is this, that they in the secular sense look upon the speaker as an actor, and the listeners as theatergoers who are to pass judgment upon the artist. But the speaker is not the actor—not in the remotest sense. No, the speaker is the prompter. There are no mere theatergoers present, for each listener will be looking into his own heart. The stage is eternity, and the listener, if he is the true listener (and if he is not, he is at fault) stands before God during the talk.[2]

What preachers do and say matters and has an impact on millennials. Preachers have the potential to speak not for themselves but for 2,000 years of tradition and experience. Preachers should proclaim Christ crucified, risen, and coming again. Preachers are needed to be both prophets and pastors from the pulpit, faithfully proclaiming the good news for the growth and strengthening of the people of God.

Preaching is an art that must be taken seriously by God's preacher. When they enter the church, whether for Sunday morning worship or for a service commemorating the life of someone they loved, millennials need a word of hope and resurrection, not judgment and condemnation. These opportunities to preach are golden opportunities for evangelism and artic-ulation of the gospel for the sake of millennials.

"Evangelism" is a dirty word to some these days, but mainline preachers have the opportunity to reclaim that word for the sake of its original intent. To be a preacher as evangelist requires a constant willingness to nudge the people of God to go on to perfection in this life. To be a preacher as evangelist requires a constant willingness to reach out to millennials on the margins who are hurt by the church and disenfranchised by the institution. To be a preacher as evangelist requires a willingness to reshape and reform the message for a new generation of Christians.

In my observations, for the millennial worshiper, relevant, meaningful, and authentic sermons are at the crux of choosing a church. If the pastor as preacher is not bringing an "A" game every Sunday, then he or she might as well not preach. Inauthentic preaching or plain bad preaching does more harm than not preaching at all.

Working with our words as wordsmiths to preach a cohesive message every Sunday can be daunting, but ultimately it is the work the preacher is called to. If ministers are serious about their calling to preach, then that calling should take precedence. In preaching, we have a captive audience like none other. The rest of our work as ministers informs our work as preachers.

The reality is that preaching should be the bread and butter of any gifted minister. Millennials need a good word of hope from their preachers. The final and ultimate question for any minister is, will you provide that in your preaching?

The Hope of Millennial Worship

The hope of millennial worship is deeper than settling wars between contemporary and traditional camps. It is in creating and authenticating valuable worship. Worship is our response to God's faithfulness. In the context of the hope of God's faithfulness, millennials will find authentic worship. Many in my generation don't want to respond in worship; we want fulfillment and instant gratification. That is simply part of who we are. But if churches begin to challenge millennials to a response-driven worship, we will see revitalization in worship and in liturgy.

Response-driven worship involves liturgical action and fulfillment of the sacraments. It involves healthy hymnody or worship music that has theological depth beyond a praise chorus and that challenges parishioners to respond in ways they might not have expected. Response-driven worship garners a new understanding of what worship means to us.

Worship is not and never has been human-centered. It is so much deeper than that. Worship is response, and while it may be fulfilling, that is not the end game of worship. Our response to God's faithfulness is a reminder that this world and this church are not ours, and that is something my generation desperately needs to remember. Though we are bound for the kingdom of God in our worship, we must always remember that we are not the object of our worship. God is. God is the reason we respond, and God's faithfulness is the reality we find ourselves in when we worship.

I am hopeful that the current state of the church in terms of declining membership and dwindling money will allow us to do some soul searching on what it means to worship authentically. We are a resurrection people, and God can bring even the church up from the ashes, but we must be faithful in our response to resurrection. It is in that mindset that we go forth in the name of the Lord, to worship and to serve, as millennials, as baby boomers, as Gen X'ers. We are bound together to worship the God who created us and the God who sustains us. May we do so in spirit and in truth.

Notes

1. Fred Pratt Green, "When in Our Music God Is Glorified," Hope Publishing Company, 1972.

2. Fred Edie, *Book, Bath, Table, Time: Christian Worship as Source and Resource for Youth Ministry* (Cleveland OH: Pilgrim Press, 2007).

3. Søren Kierkegaard, *Purity of Heart Is to Will One Thing*, trans. Douglas Steere (New York: Harper and Brothers, 1948) 180–81.

Chapter 11

REFLECTIONS FROM THE STAINED GLASS

with Palmer Cantler

The church has lasted for almost two thousand years and has not died yet. The church has survived heresies, persecution, and plague without dying. The millennial generation will not be the absolute end of the church. It just may mean the end of the church as we know it. And that is what gives me hope. —Palmer Cantler

Where do I even begin with Palmer? Palmer and I met the summer between our junior and senior years of high school. At that time we both wrestled with the concept of being "public theologians" at the Youth Theological Initiative at Candler School of Theology on the campus of Emory University. We spent a month together, and since then we have fostered in each other God's gentle calling to ministry. Palmer and I now sit beside each other in our classes at Duke, and I am confident in those moments that I am in the presence of a future bishop.

Palmer's story here reiterates that God will not give up on millennials and the church. I am confident that any church or Annual Conference that has Palmer Cantler as a part of it will survive and thrive. When our time is committed to posterity, when I face the end of my life, one of my greatest joys will have been to say, "I knew Palmer way back when."

Palmer is a second-year divinity student at Duke University Divinity School. She completed her undergraduate degree at Wofford College and is a native of Tennessee where she is a candidate for ministry in the Holston Annual Conference of the United Methodist Church.

Rob Lee: Tell me how you were called to the ministry.

Palmer Cantler: I have always grown up in the United Methodist Church. My first bottle given to me by someone other than a family member was by the lay leader of the UMC where my parents were members. I spent many days of my childhood in a port-a-crib in the church office or watching VeggieTales in the conference room. My mother worked at our local church, and I grew up exploring those halls. Through church camps, VBS, youth group events, and numerous activities, the church became an essential part of my life. My parents held leadership positions in the church and demonstrated true servant leadership. With such wonderful role models, my definition of being a successful adult became tied to being part of the church.

It was in the summer of 2006 that I first began to feel my call to ministry. While at a youth event called Assembly put on by the Holston Conference of the United Methodist Church, I was walking down the hall to sign up for an afternoon workshop. A row of posters on the wall advertised different workshops, and my attention was focused on a creative prayer poster at the end. However, my feet stopped in front of a bright green sign that screamed, "So You Want to Go into Ministry?" I could not help but mentally laugh it off with a stubborn "no." Helping in the church is one thing, but working there? No, thank you. Instead of walking towards the prayer poster, though, I felt my feet move forward, and, before I knew it, I was writing my name on that bright green poster. I remember praying that night, as a scrawny, shy seventh grader, for God to show me if this was my future. And as I've grown up, that prayer continues to echo in my mind. Yet God has helped to guide me forward and show me that I belong in ministry.

My call has not remained the same in the past ten years. I went from being solely focused on youth ministry to a desire to be ordained as an elder in the United Methodist Church and serve as a pastor. Through several internships and guidance from mentors, I have come to see how my natural leadership skills and desire to care for others play out in my ministry.

Why buy stock in a dying organization? That is to say, why are you pursuing a calling that many millennials and people your age have given up?

The short answer would be to say that I cannot see myself anywhere else. I continue to work toward a career in an organization that is dying off because none of the back-up plans I fashion can help relieve the desire in my soul to lead a congregation in worship. A short explanation is that the church is so much a part of my identity that I cannot imagine not serving in it, even when others have given up.

The long answer is actually a question: why should I run away from my calling, even if others designate it as dying? Of the many things ministry involves, one is following the stirring of the Holy Spirit. Sometimes we follow it into relationships with others who are different from us in order to foster community, and other times we follow it by taking a chance in order to reenergize the church. I recently read *I Refuse to Lead a Dying Church* by the Reverend Paul Nixon and was struck by his strong refusal of complacency. He outlines decisions a church must make in order to choose life over death, because doing the same thing as always will only lead to disaster. I feel called to ministry in the church, and I see it as part of my calling to give room for the Holy Spirit to move and revitalize the church.

How has your calling affected your relationships, friendships, and family dynamics? Are they concerned that you're interested in a precarious ministry? What is your response to them?

Let's just say it makes for an interesting conversation on a first date when you say you want to be a pastor. I've had my fair share of interesting (awkward) conversations with other millennials when I expressed my calling to work in the church. These conversations either turned into confessions or apologies, both involving why the other person hasn't been to church recently. As for family and friends, they have been largely supportive. Either they recognize my calling or choose not to say anything because I'm too headstrong.

I haven't had to deal with responding to others' concerns for my ministry, because I am open with my unhappiness about the current state of the church. I am trying to educate myself on how the church operates so that I am not trying to lead a church while I am blind to the realities it faces.

Where have you seen God in the millennial generation?

I see God in the way the millennial generation is craving to interact with the sacred. Rudolf Otto talked about how the divine is manifested in two forms: *mysterium tremendum et fascinans.* That which is holy or divine (God) both makes us both quake in fear and draw close in fascination. I think the millennial generation shares this understanding. We do not want a superficial, watered-down understanding of God. We want to interact with something that is wholly other from ourselves, and many millennials are finding that in more liturgical worship styles. We do not want to be catered to, so there is a craving for authentic worship. I see God working in the millennial generation by pulling people towards genuine relationships and a pure desire to interact with that which is mysterious.

What gives you the most hope about the church?

I find hope in the way that my generation will not settle for less than authenticity. The millennial generation is willing to call the church out on the problems that have plagued it for so long. The church has lasted for almost two thousand years and has not died yet. The church has survived heresies, persecution, and plague without dying. The millennial generation will not be the absolute end of the church. It just may mean the end of the church as we know it. And that is what gives me hope. I find hope in how the church will continue because the church is not dependent on humanity; it is dependent on God. I recently heard a Pentecost sermon that connected the energy of the first Pentecost to how the church needs to turn the page and begin a new chapter. I find hope that there is more to come in the future of the church, and I pray that I might be part of it.

Why stay? Why now? Why be a part of this movement that is slowing down?

Simply, why the hell not? Call it stubbornness or persistence, but I refuse to give up on the church that was integral to my upbringing. Part of me wants to be part of the movement to help bring energy and life back to the church. Part of me is anxiously awaiting something big to happen. I have never been good at giving up, and maybe that is why I cannot walk away. I choose to stay with the mainline Protestant church even when it might be slowing down because I'm not sure that it is time to walk away. All hope is not lost. Not yet.

What are your hopes for the future of the institutional church?

I am almost afraid to speak my hopes for the future of the institutional church because I feel as though expressing them will make them not come true, like a birthday wish. But I have great hope for the church. I cannot help having hope for the church in order to block out the anxiety that maybe I am wrong. But I want to hope that we will have another great renewal of the Spirit in the church. I don't have a specific picture for how I think the church will look on the other side of change. I just hope that I never reach a level of complacency where I might stand in the way of the Spirit.

REFLECTION QUESTIONS

1. Palmer speaks of the church surviving for 2,000 years. How have you seen the church survive in your own context?

2. Palmer was called to ministry at a young age. When did you first feel God's tug on your heart?

3. What is your wish for the church?

Chapter 12

REFRAMING THE SACRAMENTS FOR MILLENNIALS

At the font we start our journey, in the Easter faith baptized; doubts and fears no longer blind us, by the light of Christ surprised. Alleluia, alleluia! Hope held out and realized. At the altar we are nourished with the Easter gift of bread; in our breaking it to pieces see the love of Christ outspread. Alleluia, alleluia! Life embraced, yet freely shed.
—*Jeffrey Rowthorn*[1]

In chapter 10, we talked of the importance of authentic worship for millennials. We spoke of preaching and hymnody and reforming the way we worship. I wanted to be careful when talking about "reforming" the sacraments, for they do not need our consent to be constantly reforming, so this chapter was born. Have you ever been to an eye doctor and gone through the routine of seeing which lens is best for you to determine your prescription? This chapter is an attempt to do the same thing in regards to the blessed sacraments of our faith.

Millennials crave authentic worship, and what can be more authentic than a shared communal experience in which we offer our inner beings to one another? The sacraments have the potential to bring us to our core and therefore unite our souls with God. Where do we start such a journey to the center of our being? Where does a millennial like me who is invested in the church crave vulnerability and authenticity most?

At the font and at the table.

Font

At the baptismal font we start the journey of faith. We are initiated into the body of Christ and marked as Christ's own forever. Forever is a long time for millennials like myself; commitment of any kind can be hard for us. When we are invited to share in the deep mystery of baptism, we are invited to be vulnerable to our own death and weakness. Regardless of generation, this is something people don't want to face. But it is something younger generations need to be reminded of.

Death and mortality are real and they are scary. Baptism seeks to interject grace amid that mortality and death. For many in my generation, facing death gracefully is hard. We are at the forefront of medical achievement in prolonging life. We're all after the elixir of life and the sorcerer's stone that would keep us from dying. But perhaps we can look at our mortality another way.

Through baptism, we find a reforming of a millennial mindset of immortality. The words we say and the pictures we take are committed to posterity because of technological advancements. Baptism says "not so fast." Baptism is a reminder that we are called to live in accordance with the gospel. Through our initiation and witness in baptism, we become part of the community that wants to hold us in its arms through our years and greet us on the other side of the Jordan when our time is done on earth.

That's what baptism has done and should do for millennials like me: it gives perspective. It gives us perspective that we are not alone in this world and are not the fullness of this world individually. Many people who have gone before us and many generations to come after us have contributed or will contribute just as much as we have. Even though that is a sobering reality for my generation, it is one we need to hear. We hear that through diving deep into the waters of baptism.

I can't remember my own baptism. I was baptized on All Saints Day in November 1992. A two-month-old won't remember his baptism as some do, but the congregation that witnessed my baptism has told me time and time again that I was loved and accepted regardless of what would happen through the years. I even ended up leaving the denomination for a time, but when I returned I was welcomed with open arms and a loving smile.

That's what my generation needs. Simply and directly, we need to know that we are accepted. Regardless of the issues that divide our time or generations, millennials need to know that they are accepted. Paul Tillich's words could ring true for my generation:

Sometimes at that moment a wave of light breaks into our darkness, and it is as though a voice were saying: "You are accepted. You are accepted, accepted by that which is greater than you, and the name of which you do not know. Do not ask for the name now; perhaps you will find it later. Do not try to do anything now; perhaps later you will do much. Do not seek for anything; do not perform anything; do not intend anything. Simply accept the fact that you are accepted!" If that happens to us, we experience grace. After such an experience we may not be better than before, and we may not believe more than before. But everything is transformed. In that moment, grace conquers sin, and reconciliation bridges the gulf of estrangement. And nothing is demanded of this experience, no religious or moral or intellectual presupposition, nothing but acceptance.[2]

Millennials need a good word from the church. We need to hear that baptism is more than initiation into a social club in which we are told how to act or what to do. Millennials need to know that they are initiated into a group simply because they are accepted as beloved children of God. I'm not suggesting we write blank checks for people to do whatever they want, but when we reframe the conversation to make the baptized members of the Body of Christ into irreplaceable icons of a living God, then we can see how the conversation shifts. Viewed with this mindset, baptism has value and authenticity for the millennial generation.

Table

Authenticity is found around a shared meal. In Acts 2, after the Pentecost experience, Luke writes, "Day by day, as they spent much time together in the temple, they broke bread at home and ate their food with glad and generous hearts, praising God and having the goodwill of all the people. And day by day the Lord added to their number those who were being saved" (Acts 2:46-47). This mindset of a shared meal must be reclaimed and reshaped for a millennial generation. I can think of countless times when I have shared a feast outside the church with my friends and colleagues. But if we were to offer a feast in the church that provided something holy and mysterious, I believe the offering would attract millennials.

The reality is simple: we have forsaken Communion for the sake of timely and convenient worship. We want worship that ends at 12:00 p.m. on Sunday, and if Communion goes over our tightly prescribed worship times, then all hell will break loose. But worship and the sacrament of the

Eucharist should never be convenient or timely. For when the Eucharist comes into our lives, it creates, restores, and reframes our lives in a holy and existential way.

I grow increasingly skeptical of the symbolic nature of the Eucharist. People treat it as if nothing changes or happens when the minister blesses the elements of bread and wine. Granted, my view of the sacraments is high, but, nonetheless, to suggest that Communion is nothing more than a liturgical act on our way to lunch is preposterous. I'm reminded that Flannery O'Conner once remarked in regards to Communion, "If it's a symbol then to hell with it."[3]

We come to the table, sometimes with no idea why we go, and we find ourselves meeting the Creator and Redeemer of creation there. That's something millennials will support. An encounter with the living Christ is something we all seek, whether we admit it to ourselves or not. But the reality is that if we get bogged down in timely or convenient worship, the experience loses its authenticity and thus loses the interest and value millennials might glean from it.

Shared meals are important to our faith, whether they are in corporate worship or in the bar down the street from the church. Gathered at the table, we find ourselves face to face with the *imago dei* intrinsic in every human being. They invite us into an encounter with Christ and the people around us. When we eat at the feast of liturgy, we acknowledge that even in our confessions and failures we are one in the Spirit of God.

What does this mean for millennials? Have you ever tried inviting someone of my generation to share a meal? I guarantee this generation loves to share in Communion with one another and with those of different generations because we find ourselves deeply yearning for community and authenticity. At the table, we meet that community face to face.

I can vividly remember my senior minister at the first church I served taking me out to lunch with his young boys one day. Ethan, the younger of the two, shared with me the salsa and chips that came with our meal. He likened it to Communion because we were dipping chips in salsa like we did in intinction (dipping bread in wine) when we celebrated Communion. This was a holy reminder that the Eucharistic feast reaches beyond the church doors, and we can reframe Communion to look more like a meal than a holy snack at a drive-through on our way to lunch.

What Is Sacramental for You?

That story of likening Communion to chips and salsa reminds me of the importance of recognizing the sacraments in our midst that might not be recognized by the church. Many define sacraments as signs or imitations of Christ's presence in the church. But ultimately, even the church can't agree on the sacraments. For instance, while many Protestants only recognize two (Baptism and the Eucharist) others recognize more; the Catholic Church recognizes seven. Some celebrate them regularly, while others wouldn't fully understand the sacrament of Communion because their church never commemorates the passion of our Lord in that way. I find that the sacraments can be indicative of the faith we all share, especially for millennials. For some, the sacrament of life comes alive in seven to twenty to one hundred different ways, as if God's self were present with that person every moment of every hour. But then, there are others for whom the sacrament of life feels foreign. Luckily, God does not need our permission to be God, and we can see traces of sacramental living in everything we do, even if it's been too long since we last celebrated the sacraments either of the church or of life.

Where are the traces of sacramental life for you? I can remember growing up and watching the two-acre yard behind my house flood with the rains during the summer. Even when it wasn't raining, there were traces of the river that had flowed. There was a creek bed, signs of life, and the path that the roaring rains had cut through the bottom of the gulley. Dear people of faith, look for the traces, look for the hope, of sacramental living. You will see that millennials like myself crave the liturgy of the sacraments. We crave life itself and the sacrament of a life well lived. If I can find hope in the traces of the river in my backyard, then we can all find traces of hope for millennials and sacramental living.

More than Holy Goldfish

My Nana called Communion "holy goldfish" because she felt that people would go down for a snack before they rushed off to their Sunday lunch reservations. Later, in my undergrad studies, I wrote a research paper on the mysteries of the sacraments. I wanted to see if people really knew what they were asking for when they went to the font and to the table.

The results were striking. People realized that however mysterious the sacrament may be for them, it was indeed a holy moment. Most of my survey participants found a great benefit in receiving and remembering the sacraments. This data was translatable across the generations, but what was impressive was that millennials felt it as well. Grace abounds in the sacraments for people of every age. What can millennials and people who minister to millennials learn from this?

Take the sacraments seriously. An authentic, vulnerable, community-driven view of sacramental theology is necessary not only for church reformation but also for the inbreaking of the kingdom of God. This is accomplished through attention to the sacraments of the church, coupled with signs and symbols of sacramental living. We must find means and realities of grace in our daily lives as well as in our community's life. The sacraments remind us that things made from wheat, grapes, and the elements of hydrogen and oxygen are important to God. Or, as my friend Broderick Greer says, "Matter matters to God." Communion is so much more than holy goldfish snacks; it is an encounter with God. I've often found myself wanting to take off my shoes before the celebration of the sacraments, for we are indeed standing on holy ground.

Does this sound romanticized or too good to be true? For some, perhaps. But I once heard Father Greg Boyle, SJ, give a lecture at Duke where he said, "We believe in a God who is too good to be true, and when humans bump up against something we think is too good to be true we refuse to believe that it is." Part of sacramental theology for millennials is reminding ourselves and others that we bump up against God when have the common meal of Communion or baptize someone and mark them as Christ's own forever. Deeper than that, we realize that God does not need our consent to be God, and we are invited into the sacramental way of living regardless of what we know to be true about ourselves and our doubts.

This Holy Mystery

In one of the Eucharistic prayers in my denomination, we say, "We give you thanks for this holy mystery, in which you have given yourself to us." Ultimately, millennials need an invitation into the divine mystery of the sacraments. We need to be told that the church doesn't have it all figured out, and that is where grace happens. In that precise moment—the moment of mystery when the bread and wine are lifted up or the prayer is spoken over the water—we have a profound reminder that we don't have it all figured out. What kind of God would invite those who rejected God to a banquet or to an opportunity to be marked forever in the light of Christ?

A professor once asked me to write a paper on the topic, "What kind of God would call you to ministry?" To be honest, that God must be a little off the holy rocker to call generation after generation of ill-equipped people to vocational ministry. But perhaps God is calling millennials to invest in the church in order to save them. Many a time, God has called people to ministry to save them from themselves. For the sake of their salvation, God has called them to a holy mystery. How odd and exciting is that? A sacramental God is a God who takes commonplace things and makes them holy.

If we're going to get serious about reenvisioning the sacraments, we must take seriously the work we do in the holy mystery of God. If we're going to remind millennials of the importance of bread and wine around a table of grace, then we must first be willing to go there ourselves—not out of obligation or a sense of responsibility, but as people who want to become what we consume.

Notes

1. Jeffrey Rowthorn, "At the Font We Start Our Journey," Hope Publishing Company, 1991.

2. Paul Tillich, "You Are Accepted," in *The Shaking of Foundations* (1948; repr., Eugene OR: Wipf & Stock Publishing, 2012).

3. Flannery O'Connor, *The Habit of Being: Letters of Flannery O'Connor* (New York: Vintage Books, 1980).

Chapter 13

REFLECTIONS FROM THE STAINED GLASS

with Brent Murphy

Truth be told, ministry, in and of itself, is the definition of risk! However, what would ministry be without faith, and how would faith function without risk? —Brent Murphy

Brent Murphy and I don't always see eye to eye, but I consider him a wonderful friend. In part *because of* our differences, his voice is important to this book. In the next few pages, you'll be hearing from someone who is currently serving in the Pentecostal tradition. I've attended Brent's mostly millennial church in Greensboro, North Carolina, and there is beauty in seeing a group of young adults worshiping God together.

As you read this, may you be challenged, as I have, to find friends who may not agree with everything you think. They may become cherished friends with whom to float ideas and concepts. There is beauty in tension, so let's be bold enough to claim it.

Brent is a second-year divinity student at Duke University Divinity School. He is currently the pastor of New Birth Bible Fellowship in Raleigh, North Carolina.

Rob Lee: Tell me how you were called to the ministry.

Brent Murphy: The stories of Moses, Isaiah, Samuel, and Abraham are some of the most well-known biblical narratives. These stories share a common motif: God appeared to the individuals, called them, and sent them forward into the work of ministry! The beauty in these stories lies not only in the calling from God but also in the struggles, problems, and imperfections of the called that lead up to the calling of God! I fit into this mix. My call story begins with a few problems, struggles, and personal imperfections.

I spent most of my childhood traveling between a triangle of custody—my mother, my maternal grandmother, and my maternal aunt. My mother spent most of my adolescent life incarcerated. In an attempt to take care of my sister and me, my mother chose her children over what was legal. This was the beginning of the custody triangle. My sister and I lived with my grandmother for a few years. Many psychologists would call these years the formative years. It was during this time of formation that I developed faith in the Lord, Jesus Christ.

Being raised in church became the foundation defining my life. Unlike other children, when asked in first and second grade about places I wanted to go, people I wanted to be, and things I wanted to do, all of my answers were laced with Christian colloquialisms. Church was everything to me. While church meant the world to me on one hand, on the other hand my life was in disarray. After my sister and I lived with my grandmother for a while, my mother got out of prison. A year passed, and then she went back again. This would happen four times through my adolescent, preteen, and teenage years.

Depression, pornographic addiction, self-esteem wars, and many other difficulties were a byproduct of the emotional instability of my childhood. To this day, I credit my emotional stability to the formation of my faith at Mount Livingstone United Holy Church, my grandmother's church!

What does this have to with my call to ministry? Simply put, everything! Upon the beginning of my freshman year at North Carolina A&T, I was sitting in the lobby eavesdropping on a conversation. The young lady, speaking to the group she was sitting with, talked about issues that seemed to consume her because of her mother's incarceration. As I listened, my spirit awakened, and I invited myself into the conversation. I spoke to her about my experience and encouraged her to hold on to her faith. Then the young lady said to me, "You should start a Bible study!" Hearing this, I responded in the affirmative, not realizing what God was beginning to do in me.

As I walked to my room that evening, I begin to think back over my life. I thought, "Wow, this must've been the reason I endured such hurt! God, you must've been preparing me for this night." When I got to my room, I picked up my Bible. I opened it, prepared to read whatever it turned to. To my surprise, the book opened to Luke 4:18: "The Spirit of the Lord is upon me, because he has anointed me to bring good news to the poor. He has sent me to proclaim release to the captives and recovery of sight to the blind, to let the oppressed go free." It was in reading what Jesus said that I able to acknowledge my call to ministry and preaching!

Why buy stock in a dying organization? That is to say, why are you pursuing a calling that many millennials and people your age have given up?

I feel called, specifically, to this generation. I believe God has gifted us with the wisdom of the generations before us, and we have the innovation of the current and successive generations to help bridge the gap. In my denomination, the United Holy Church of America, INC (UHCA), which is a predominately holiness/Pentecostal reformation, it seems as if one is only qualified to lead, pastor, or become bishop at the age of seventy. In answering my call, I believe God has called me to help be one of the agents of change to resurrect the church. The church will not die as long as there are individuals with hearts humble enough to listen and brave enough to act!

How has your calling affected your relationships, friendships, and family dynamics? Are they concerned that you're interested in a precarious ministry? What is your response to them?

Many have told me, straight to my face (how noble of them), that God did not call me to plant a church! When I first felt the yearning to move toward planting a church, as any person would do, I talked it over with people I trusted for advice. Many of them said affirmative things while others did not. In *Launch*, the authors state, "If you can be talked out of planting a church, you're not called to plant a church!" In reading this, my attitude shifted; I knew God had called me, and I was not willing to let anything get in the way of following that call. Many relationships with previous confidants were destroyed, but many new meaningful relationships burgeoned, fostering an environment of challenge and support to my calling. To be honest, I can understand why some of them disagreed with me. It speaks to the second half of your question. They thought doing this was precarious. Truth be told, ministry, in and of itself, is the definition of risk! However, what would ministry be without faith, and how would faith function without risk?

Where have you seen God in the millennial generation?

The fact that God is omnipresent suggests that wherever we are, God is! That statement, along with the expression of God in the Trinity, exemplifies God in consistent motion in and through our lives. To be more specific, I've found in the last few months that God is at work in doubt, confusion, and myths about the faith. Millennials are full of questions, some even unanswerable: Can God be wrong? Why does evil exist if God is good? Why do I need to attend church? What makes Christianity the only right way? These are questions I've been asked over the last few months. While at one point in time I would have rebuked the person for speaking that way about God, I now see things in a different light. In the story about Philip and the Ethiopian eunuch, the eunuch had a question, and God sent Philip to answer that question in the heat of the day, in the hottest place—the desert. In this story, I see millennials wanting to believe but not enough people willing to go out in the hottest and driest places to reach and teach them. The fact that they're reaching illuminates the work of God in them!

What gives you the most hope about the church?

Simply put, I have hope because the church belongs to God. As long as the church is built on the confession of Peter, "Thou art the Christ, son of the living God," I don't think we have anything to worry about (Matt 16:16). If we believe the words of Jesus, we know that the gates of hell may burn around, through, and in the church at times, yet they won't prevail!

Why stay? Why now? Why be a part of this movement that is slowing down?

The movement will continue to slow down if our generation doesn't speed up! Our churches, though there are many things about them that need to change, will survive if we begin to stand up. This goes back to my statement from earlier. We can help our church move forward if we humble ourselves to hear the wisdom of the generations before us. After we do that, we should begin to present ideas that are innovative and faithful to our traditions. Innovation can be youthful, vibrant, and faithful to tradition all at the same time. But yes—before you ask—that's a lot harder than it sounds!

What are your hopes for the future of the institutional church?

In my tradition, the word "church" was used to refer to the people of God. It was used to separate the profane from the sanctified, the clean from the unclean, the saved from the sinner. With that, my definition of the word "church" is multifaceted. So, in thinking about my hopes for the institutional church, I look at it from a multifaceted point of view. For the church as a people, my prayer is that the church would remain faithful and bold in the face of things that defy God's word. For the church as a denomination, my hope is that God will sustain it through the politics, greed, and pride that have crept in. For the church as the body of Christ, my hope is that we would remain the church, a called-out people, sanctified, and, in the words of my grandmother quoting from 2 Timothy 2:21, "meet for my master's use."

REFLECTION QUESTIONS

• How has your story led you to serve in the context of which you are a part?
• How is the church multifaceted? What are your hopes for the institution?
• Do you have a close friend with whom you are able to disagree?

Chapter 14

RETHINKING THE ISSUES OF THE CHURCH IN RESPONSE TO MILLENNIALS

Blest be the God of Israel, who comes to set us free; who visits and redeems us, who grants us liberty. The prophets spoke of mercy, of freedom and release; God shall fulfill that promise and bring the people peace. On those who sit in darkness the sun begins to rise, the dawning of forgiveness upon the sinner's eyes. God guides the feet of pilgrims along the paths of peace. O bless our God and Savior with songs that never cease! —Michael Perry[1]

In the Dead Sea Scrolls, the Qumran Community Rule speaks of the spirit of deceit that is in this world. It suggests that one of the traits of that spirit is sluggishness in the service of justice.[2] The idea that people are sluggish to serve justice is a primary theme in this chapter. For too long, the church has been viewed as a judgmental institution that wants nothing to do with LGBTQ people, people experiencing poverty and homelessness, those with mental health concerns—anyone who is viewed as the "other." While some people consider this subject contentious, it is on the minds of millennials.

I must confess that I write with some trepidation about how we might reform some of the issues of the church. The reality is that these issues are polarizing, and they captivate the minds and hearts of so many that they become the hope on which we stake our claims of faith. To some, you are either a liberal mainline Protestant or a conservative fundamentalist Evangelical. But what we find in many millennials is that, like preceding generations, they actually have a wide variety of viewpoints and particularities. The hope of this chapter is found not in how we can reform the church to be pro-LGBTQ or anti-abortion but in the discussions that can come from these realities faced by our society and churches.

Let's go on a journey with Ruth and Naomi to Bethlehem in Judah after the death of Ruth's husband and father-in-law (see Ruth 1). Ruth is given the choice to turn away from or turn toward her destiny. She responds to Naomi's requests to turn back with this poetic answer: "Do not press me to leave you or to turn back from following you! Where you go, I will go; where you lodge, I will lodge; your people shall be my people, and your God my God. Where you die, I will die—there will I be buried. May the LORD do thus and so to me, and more as well, if even death parts me from you!" (Ruth 1:16-17). Ultimately we are all on this road together. All of us, from ardent liberal to fastidious conservative, want what's best for our church. The question is, Will we turn toward the destiny of the church? Or will we turn back to avoid controversy? The choice is ours.

Reshaping the Issues that Divide Us

If we're going to be like Ruth, turning toward the issues of the church instead of away from them, then perhaps we should start by acknowledging that the debates over issues in our church are ultimately about *people*. If we reshape the issues to be more about caring for people and what they face, then these issues would take on a different form. We would be less likely to condemn and more likely to speak truth in love. If we're going to reclaim the millennial generation for the church, we must realize that culture has moved on in many respects regarding the divisiveness that plagues us in today's church. That's not to say that the church should follow culture in every respect, but we should acknowledge that if we're going to discuss the hot-button issues faithfully, we must do it in light of today's generational lenses. We must be willing to discuss whether God is calling us toward something new and different for the sake of something big on the horizon. Perhaps God has called us to be people who insist on change for the sake of the future and for the sake of millennials. But if we're going to insist on shifting a bulky institution like the church, we'll have to do it at the place where we all can meet: at the table.

Let Us Break Bread Together on Our Knees

I have always suggested that if we want to meet each other and have good conversation about the future of the church in regard to millennials, we should do so in the fellowship of breaking bread and sharing wine. We must be the people who are willing to come to the table and lay down our swords and shields so that we might have fruitful conversations about the future of the hotly contested issues of the church. Who knows? Perhaps we could shed new light on people of faith who have a different sexual orientation than we do, or how to care properly for people experiencing homelessness or chronic mental illness. Perhaps we could have meaningful table fellowship around what it means to be a pro-life or pro-choice person of faith. Perhaps we could come to know in our hearts that the Black Lives Matter movement is a movement the church should support instead of shunning. I'm not suggesting that we abandon everything we've come to know to be true about ourselves or our faith. I am suggesting, though, that God can do a new thing in our lives for the sake of God's incredible future.

Ultimately, when we break bread together, our differences become dim in the light of God's grace. I am reminded that God came not to divide us based on generational monikers but to break bread with us, to shine light on the frailty and beauty of human existence, and to fill our desperate need for redemption.

I'm reminded of the story of Cleopas, his companion, and Jesus on the road to Emmaus (see Luke 24). Jesus is recognizable not in a theological conversation about Scripture but in a simple meal with friends. This profound moment with the resurrected Jesus rings true in some Eucharistic liturgies when the reading states, "Be known to us in the breaking of the bread." If Jesus really is the Christ, then we have a duty to break bread as those who have encountered God. We must treat these issues, these differences, and the people we disagree with in a different way, a better way, a holy way.

Waiting on the World to Change

While I've discussed how we should treat people, I haven't confronted the issues and arguments in their own right. I grew up hearing John Mayer's song, "Waiting on the World to Change." In the song, Mayer sings, "Now we see everything that's going wrong with the world and those who lead it, and we just feel like we don't have the means to rise above and beat it. So we keep waiting, waiting on the world to change." If that isn't a millennial anthem, I don't know what is.

In our millennial mindset, we see that there is so much going on, so much hurt, so much pain, but without the backing of previous generations who will face and discuss these issues with us, I wonder if anything will ever get done. In spite of the bleak issues of our time, millennials must be enabled to examine these issues and formulate a response for their generation. Millennials now outnumber baby boomers, and soon they will be the standard-bearers for our world. In that reality, the church must yield its power to millennial voices and face current issues with faith that God is still working.

The problem many people have with the church is that it is judgmental, hypocritical, and anti-LGBTQ. What is sad is that this is not the church I have come to know. It is not the church by which I have come to know Jesus Christ. Unfortunately, the narrative we hear is a grim reminder that the church is not always what it should be. For the sake of the gospel, for the sake of millennials, and for the sake of the church, we have to reform the realities of our conversations. We can no longer wait on the world to change. We have to interject change and grace into our broken and hurting world.

Confronting Privilege for What It Is

As a white, cisgender male (that is, my gender is aligned with my biological sex), I don't pretend to have ever experienced injustice like other groups have. We all need to claim and confront our places and types of privilege when discussing these issues intergenerationally and with our peers. In a millennial mindset, it is important to acknowledge generational privilege as well. On too many occasions, millennial young people have been welcomed to the table as tokens. For too long, millennial voices have been undervalued. If the church began to value the voice and role of millennials in their respective callings, then breaking bread over issues wouldn't be such a big deal. It would become beautifully commonplace in the reality of our lives.

A while back I had the opportunity to hear author and theologian Rob Bell at a venue here in Durham. We had the chance to ask questions, and

I asked him what he felt we should be talking about in seminary that may not be talked about in the ivory towers of institutions. Bell's response was remarkable: "You have to give 97 percent of yourself to this work, but in reality the stuff you're learning is great. You can read all you want about liberation theology, but there is a single mother out there who just doesn't care. It's your job to care for her and liberate her. We need all of yourself, and if it takes 43 percent of your time slogging through the junk that doesn't matter, you're missing the point."

Bell's point is that until we are willing to push for the liberation of normal, everyday people, we are missing the point of theological conversations. We are called to be people who acknowledge our privilege across generational barriers and liberate each other for a brighter tomorrow.

For too long the church has been running toward the reality of becoming an empire that Jesus warned us about. As with any empire, we, the church, believe we hold the keys to heaven and earth as a means to control and contain the movement of the Spirit. We have fought to keep the beauty of the sweet, sweet Spirit in this place because the Spirit offers a voice and gives life to the truths that threaten and bring down empires.

Tear It Down

I have a friend who is currently studying in the Marriage and Family Therapy program at Appalachian State. I visited her recently, and we got on the topic—as preachers and therapists often do—of being our most authentic selves. She made a profound comment about the human experience: "Authenticity lies in acknowledging the conflict within." I couldn't agree more and would go even further to say that experience of human authenticity rings true in the church as well.

We, the church, must reach out to millennials in an authentic way; that has been the crux of this book. But to be authentic and begin to tear down the empire we have built for the sake of human advancement, we must begin to acknowledge the conflict within the confines of the church. I am reminded of John Wesley's words in a sermon he preached titled "Catholic Spirit." He said, "But although a difference in opinions or modes of worship may prevent an entire external union, yet need it prevent our union in affection? Though we cannot think alike, may we not love alike? May we not be of one heart, though we are not of one opinion? Without all doubt, we may."[3]

To be authentic across the conflicts and across denominations means acknowledging that we do not think alike—that we have varying opinions on issues, people, and Christian teaching. In my own denomination, it seems that every four years at General Conference, the top legislative body of the United Methodist Church, we debate which people are "compatible" or "incompatible" with Christian teaching. All of this is based on hot-button issues that often coincide with societal and cultural norms.

What if we instead turned our hearts, minds, and powers toward the revitalization of the church into its fullest vision? What if we reached out in fellowship and broke bread together? Cleopas and his companion walk the road to Emmaus with Jesus, but they don't know him until he breaks bread with them. Only then do they realize that their hearts were "burning within them." Don't we have the potential to do the same?

Let me put it in universal terms. I am a Duke Blue Devils basketball fan. I love Duke basketball. But I served a beautiful church in the mountains, and one of the parishioners in that church is engaged to a famous basketball player of Duke's rival team, UNC-Chapel Hill. One evening I joined them for dinner and we broke bread together. We focused not on whose team we thought was better or who would make it to the NCAA National Championship next year. Instead, we broke bread together and shared stories in which we found common threads of grace, truth, and light. If that seems trite to you, you clearly have never lived in North Carolina.

In all seriousness, though, it's hard for you to be mad or angry at a millennial for the destruction of the institutional church if you break bread with them. In fact, I think you would be hard-pressed not to find commonalities with millennials as you share a meal with them. The same goes with reforming and reshaping the issues and controversies in the institution we know as church. Couldn't God do a mighty work in the church if we were simply willing to break bread with the people who have disagreed with us and our respective issues? I'm not advocating allowing harassment or abuse on the part of either side, but breaking bread together tears down the walls we have worked so hard to build. That may be scary, but it is also good news.

Narnia and Edenton Street Church

In C. S. Lewis's *The Lion, The Witch, and the Wardrobe,* one line sticks out to me. Susan is asking Mr. Beaver what he thinks of Aslan, the great lion and Christlike figure in the book. She asks, "Is he—quite safe?" Mr. Beaver responds, "Who said anything about safe? 'Course he isn't safe. But he's good."[4] Christ isn't safe, and the risks we take as Christians to be more like Christ require us to reshape the issues we face by loving as Christ did.

My first sermon at Edenton Street United Methodist Church was a risk. It happened in the middle of the 2016 General Conference of the United Methodist Church, and though I had concerns about the conference and even felt the gentle nudge of the Spirit of God to give voice to them, I avoided the topic at all costs in my sermon preparation. I felt that, to maintain the unity of the church and my reputation as a minister, I had to avoid any sense of misunderstanding or "taking sides" with one group or the other. Though I'm clear on where I stand, I wasn't sure if the pulpit was the place to articulate that message.

But the Christ who stands in the midst of these issues calls those who are invested to be more than preachers; Christ calls us to be *prophets*. I'm reminded of one of my favorite books: *Blood Done Sign My Name* by Timothy Tyson. Tyson's father, the Reverend Dr. Vernon Tyson, served as a pastor at a Methodist church in Oxford, North Carolina, during the height of racial tensions in the 1970s. In one part, Timothy remarks about Vernon (who ironically attends Edenton Street United Methodist Church), "Every minister worthy of the name has to walk the line between prophetic vision and spiritual sustenance, between telling people the comforting things they want to hear and challenging them with the difficult things they need to hear."[5]

So in those moments at Edenton Street Church as I stepped up to preach, I had a choice: should I be pastoral or should I be prophetic? It is my hope that I chose both. I hope that in those moments I towed the line of pastoral love and prophetic witness. These two things—prophetic witness and pastoral love—are what we have to give to millennials and to countless others through our voices and through our callings to Christian and vocational ministry. We root ourselves deep in the love of God and the hope of the world made known in Jesus Christ. In that rooting and in that reality, we see that these issues are not just about issues. They are about livelihoods and people. They are not issues on a page in discipline or by-laws, but instead people with names, faces, and realities. All the people of the millennial generation want is a place at the table where they too can break bread, share wine, and figure out where all of this is headed.

Closing Time

As I write this, I can't get Semisonic's song from the late nineties called "Closing Time" out of my head. This has been a difficult chapter to write or to tie up with a nice bow. It's partly because millennials cover a wide range of political and theological understandings. (This is evidenced by the "Reflections from the Stained Glass" sections contained within these pages.) But I think that makes these issues all the more real and pressing for us to address in healthy and holy ways.

For the millennial generation, we were formed in a time where 9/11 shaped the geopolitical, social, and cultural norms and issues. Many of us only have distant memories of times when the United States and her allies were not at war. We are formed and shaped by this reality. It is because of this that many millennials are skeptical that the church (or anyone for that matter) will be able to handle the seismic issues our religious and secular culture faces.

But this is precisely where the church can do its best work. The church can reform these issues and make them about the people the church serves. It can be a place where all are welcome regardless of who God created them to be. Perhaps when our time is committed to posterity, we will be leaner but not meaner. When we go down in the annals of history, it is my hope that the millennials who invested in the church may not be seen as those who shepherded a beautiful institution to its death but as those who, by the power of the Holy Spirit, inspired a new generation to experience the Triune God.

It is my belief that God is a big God—so big that we don't have to hold the same opinions of God to be in the same tent of fellowship with one another. If we know God at all, we know that God is a God of misfits and mishaps, constantly reforming, reshaping, redoing, and, most important, redeeming the entirety of creation, especially humanity.

In that redemption of creation and humanity, we see the beauty of these issues becoming not so much issues as they are conversations around the breaking of bread. In this mindset, LGBTQ rights, abortion, mental health, homelessness, poverty, racial justice, and countless other issues will move from being "hot button issues" to being conversations. If we can begin to break bread together, to share each other's burdens, pains, and grief, then we may find a deeper movement of the Spirit in the church we love so dearly. May we be bold enough to be honest with ourselves and with others about where we stand, but may we be humble enough to journey once more into the breach and find God there.

Notes

1. Michael Perry, "Blest Be the God of Israel," The Jubilate Group (admin. by Hope Publishing Company), 1973.

2. Florentino García Martínez and Eibert J. C. Tigchelaar, *The Dead Sea Scrolls Study Edition*, vol. 1 (New York: Brill, 1997).

3. John Wesley, "Catholic Spirit," sermon 39, text from 1872 edition, ed. Thomas Jackson, available at http://www.umcmission.org/Find-Resources/ John-Wesley-Sermons/Sermon-39-Catholic-Spirit (accessed 21 October 2016).

4. C. S. Lewis, *The Lion, the Witch, and the Wardrobe* (New York: Macmillan, 1950).

5. Timothy Tyson, *Blood Done Sign My Name* (New York: Crown Publishers, 2004).

Chapter 15

REFLECTIONS FROM THE STAINED GLASS

with Kelsey Lewis

My hope is that the institutional church would find its place among the broken rather than the powerful. There have been many casualties in the church's engagement in culture wars. In an attempt to fight back against pluralism, the church's exclusivity has wounded many. My hope is that many churches will find their niche as sanctuaries for those on the fringes. —Kelsey Lewis

It was a sunny day at Duke University when I first met Kelsey. Though she's a student at Candler School of Theology at Emory University, she was visiting for the day and we had lunch. I was struck by her story—how she managed to persevere through what many would consider a "faith crisis" and find fresh expressions of God's grace amid a sea of doubt and confusion. Most of us spend time in our lives picking up the pieces that have been broken, and Kelsey has done just that.

Her story gives me hope and speaks to the resolve and fortitude that millennials who are invested in the church have. The ragtag group that chooses to stay and fight for the institution they love may be deterred, but they will never stop. May we all take a lesson from Kelsey and begin the slow march toward the fountain of hope found in Christ our Lord.

Kelsey Lewis is a graduate of the University of South Carolina, has served as a missionary, and is a divinity student at Candler School of Theology in Atlanta, Georgia.

Rob Lee: Tell me how you were called to the ministry.

Kelsey Lewis: It's all Josh Groban's fault I'm going to be a pastor. Like many of my colleagues, my call to ministry wasn't so much a realization as it was a string of connected interests and events and discoveries that somehow led me to seminary. And that string of events starts with Josh Groban. You know, the dashing young Pavarotti-esque musician who sings "You Raise Me Up"? I developed a fangirl crush on him in the eighth grade and decided to learn Italian and Spanish so that I could understand his lyrics, which led to an interest in foreign language and culture that would last me through high school and beyond.

It landed me at the University of South Carolina, where I went to study international business with grandiose ideas of being a jetsetter, shopping in Paris, and drinking cappuccinos in Rome. However, it wasn't long into my freshman year that I realized I only had interest in the international side of the international business equation. While I stuck with the field of study, I found my vocational goals slipping from my heart's grip. That year I attended a Christian conference themed around foreign missions and evangelism. Realizing that my language ability made me valuable to the mission field, I signed up for a short-term summer trip to Peru with the Baptist Collegiate Ministry, hoping to use my gifts to give back to others and to God.

I fell in love. With Latin America. With Spanish. But mostly with serving the Lord in the big, beautiful world God created. Every summer of my college career was spent in rural Central and South American villages, my hands and feet dirty and my heart happy. As my senior year of college rolled around, I knew that foreign missions was not something I was going to simply get out of my system, and I applied and was accepted into a two-year international missionary program.

I got a job doing a demographic research project in Buenos Aires, Argentina—a diverse urban megacity unlike any Latin America I knew. The day-to-day of my job there consisted mainly of doing surveys in each neighborhood of the city, gathering demographic and faith statistics that the census there did not assess. The data was (1) used to strategize American missionary involvement in the city and (2) shared with local churches so that they might better understand the faith makeup of their own neighborhoods. Home of the beloved Pope Francis, Buenos Aires is a diverse megacity with Catholicism running through its veins like water in the River Plate running along its border. (That is to say, there's a lot of water in it, but there's a lot of other stuff in it too.) While the results weren't terribly surprising, the work took an unexpected toll on me.

I grew up a conservative Southern Baptist in the American South. My upbringing wasn't so different from that of my Argentine survey takers. Going to church was not something I chose for myself. Like that of the Argentine Catholics, my faith was so closely intertwined with my culture and family life that it was hardly something I questioned as a child. My church involvement had been the source of so much comfort and positive formation—it had led me to the mission field, after all! But the stories I heard from people every day in Argentina opened my eyes to the dark side of church involvement. The truth that resounded from the surveys was that the large majority of Argentines in Buenos Aires, despite having grown up under heavy church influence, were either no longer practicing or no longer believers at all. And from what I heard on a daily basis, it was a result of bad personal experiences at church or with people of faith. These stories weighed heavily on me. I'd had such good experiences with the ministries I had participated in . . . until about eighteen months into my two-year term.

Unexpected conflict arose when my American supervisor falsely accused me of hiding a relationship with my very not-secret boyfriend. I had met an American guy my age vacationing in Argentina and begun a relationship with him a few weeks prior to the confrontation. I was transparent about it. I was a sheltered church girl with zero dating experience, so I confided in my supervisor's wife as I navigated this uncharted territory. For whatever reason, she didn't tell her husband about the relationship and it looked like I had hidden it. I tearfully apologized for the miscommunication, thinking it was simply a misunderstanding that we could work through. A continent away from my own family, I had spent Thanksgiving, Christmas, and birthdays with these folks. They were family to me. But now my supervisor was throwing around ugly, untrue accusations, denigrating my work and my character. I had been so fearful of having my heart broken by this new boy in my life that I had never thought to protect myself from my own faith family. After three miserable weeks of prayer and fasting, I turned in my letter of resignation and returned to the United States without saying good-bye to my Argentine friends. I didn't know what to tell any of them.

Bouncing back from that event took time. In retrospect, I see now that the surveys I did on the streets of Argentina, hearing all those painful and heavy stories, had prepared my heart for my personal experience. It's often easier to see God's love for other people as real and valid than it is to accept it for oneself. Hearing the hurts of other people at the hands of people of faith was what helped me to separate the merciful and righteous character of God from the actions of the flawed people who represent God, and it shined a light on my own heart, helping me to reflect on the ways I had unknowingly hurt others in Christ's name.

I believe that experience helped me to see Christ in the burned out and marginalized people of the church. It made me a better listener. And it cultivated in me a desire to heal the wounds inflicted by false gospels, by rejection, and by shame.

The Christian church places a lot of emphasis on the personal testimony, but we do so in a way that highlights the victorious stories with happy resolutions. We often forget that the rest of the world has a testimony to tell too. For every Jacob there is an Esau. For every Sarah there is a Hagar. My call to ministry came from finding myself in the camp of Esau and Hagar, from hearing their stories and seeing how deeply Yahweh loves them too. What will we do for Hagar and Esau?

Why buy stock in a dying organization? That is to say, why are you pursuing a calling that many millennials and people your age have given up?

We have all heard the millennial buzzword in regards to faith: authenticity. But I think the deeper level of our generation's search for faith is contained in another word: disillusionment. Our generation has been exposed to an unprecedented amount of heartache. Formative events that shaped our childhood include the terrorist attacks of 9/11, the Iraq war, the greatest recession since the Great Depression, and the world of the Internet that opens us up to such phenomena as catfishing, cyberbullying, stalking, child predation, and the whole gamut of danger. Fear and distrust have been forged into us by exposure to these dangers.

We are increasingly disillusioned with the power of our institutions, in both the public and private sectors, to create a just society in which humanity can flourish in security. The human heart longs for equality and justice, the same ideals of our previous generations, and we have found that the institutions in which we have placed our hope have failed us because they are composed of flawed human beings, unable to protect us or work for the good of us all.

I have bought stock in the church because, in spite of our skepticism, we desperately crave the safety of the community of God and God's people. And because I deeply believe the church may yet sing the chorus that turns the ears of a hurting world to the saving, redeeming love of Christ, who alone can reconcile and redeem our broken hearts, broken neighborhoods, and broken world.

How has your calling affected your relationships, friendships, and family dynamics? Are they concerned that you're interested in a precarious ministry? What is your response to them?

While there are no female clergy in my family, I have the benefit of having strong, intelligent women of God in my life, on both my maternal and paternal sides. My decision to go into the ministry has been met with support. Like many others in my generation, I grew up hearing that I could do anything I put my mind to. Nobody told me about the asterisk the conservative complementarian church put on that statement for little girls until I was in my twenties and already butting up against the "glass steeple." It was a painful realization that the calling to share the gospel that had been on my heart was not going to be possible in the context in which my faith was formed. My family has felt that pain with me.

Where have you seen God in the millennial generation?

One of the most formative moments in my ministry has been witnessing the response of the church after the 2015 Charleston Emmanuel AME Church shooting that made the world turn and cry with my hometown. I was born and raised in Charleston and was shaken by the nearness of the tragedy as the small city mourned the loss of nine black Christian martyrs at the hands of a white supremacist.

The church I attended was one a few that responded immediately by organizing a prayer vigil for the whole city to be able to pray collectively for the families and for our hurting world, still so plagued by the evil of racism. Abel's blood cried out from the ground that day, and we stopped to listen and mourn.

Over three thousand people came to that prayer service, and the whole city stood still for nine minutes as all the church bells rang in unison to honor the dead. That day I held hands with strangers and prayed for reconciliation to fall upon our city. I prayed for forgiveness for the sins of my ancestors. I prayed for healing for the grieving families and for the people of

South Carolina. And I prayed for unity. Afterward we all walked a block to Mother Emanuel AME, surrounded the church, and sang "Amazing Grace" to its walls. Later that night, over 10,000 people walked the Ravenel Bridge, forming a unity chain, hand in hand with strangers of various races.

I saw strangers embrace each other, cry together, and pray together. I saw white Christians recognize that purging the evil from within our borders starts with purging it from our own hearts. I saw black Christians respond with incredible grace. For the first time, as I gathered with more than three thousand strangers for prayer in the 100-degree heat, I saw God at work in Charleston, breathing life into death.

I saw the gospel personified in Charleston that day. Into utter darkness, God inserted God's presence: "let there be light." Out of death and despair sprang life and hope. Out of the mouths of the wounded and grieving came confounding words of unmerited forgiveness. It was a moment I will never forget as long as I live.

What gives you the most hope about the church?

Christ finishes the Great Commission with "I am with you always" (Matt 28:20). That's what gives me the most hope about the church. The church, just like any other human institution, is flawed. But the resurrected Christ who defeated death promises his presence to us.

This is the same One who made our earth from nothing, beginning with "let there be light." This is the same One who formed us from the dust and who revives a valley of dry bones. Those dry bones in Ezekiel are a reminder to me that we may be broken, even lifeless, but nothing is beyond God's redemption. We are those dry bones. As the church, we too are raised to walk in newness of life because of the enduring presence of a Christ who did it first.

Why stay? Why now? Why be a part of this movement that is slowing down?

I've been fortunate to be a part of some fantastic ministries and to witness church done well: communities that build each other up and care for the downtrodden among them.

I owe much of my leadership skill to Tim Stewart, my college minister at the University of South Carolina's Baptist Collegiate Ministry where I served as president. Tim saw potential in me and encouraged me to mentor others, teach, and lead.

Awaken Church in Charleston, South Carolina, was my church home after I returned from Argentina. It was the place where God truly healed my heart from the pain I experienced on the mission field. The church was barely a year old when I first started attending. What makes Awaken a truly special church is that instead of being centered on Sundays, it is centered around small groups. The "main event" of Awaken is the weekly groups that meet in people's homes. While the Sunday morning services are well run and bear great fruit, Awaken knows that relationships formed in home groups are helpful for sustaining a more genuine community. When the group I attended outgrew the leader's living room, he asked me to lead my own in my home. Leading that group of young adults every week helped me realize my call to ministry in a tangible way and taught me how to be faithful with a little, in preparation to be faithful with a lot.

The common thread running through these two ministries is that they place great value on equipping leaders to be the hands and feet of Christ. The USC BCM was largely student run and organized, and it provided opportunities for different students to lead as another senior class graduated each year. Awaken invested its time and resources into their small-group leaders, making them mini pastors of their flocks.

Ministries like these are bright spots in my faith that remind me that the church still has a place in our culture and still has the ability to thrive and meet the needs of the communities in which they are situated.

What are your hopes for the future of the institutional church?

My hope is that the institutional church will find its place among the broken rather than the powerful. There have been many casualties in the church's engagement culture wars. In an attempt to fight back against pluralism, the church's exclusivity has wounded many. My hope is that many churches will find their niche as sanctuaries for those on the fringes. It is my prayer that in this, we can develop a theology of suffering that focuses on the crucified Christ, who also suffered at the hand of the religious elite. This is the kind of faith that weathers suffering and tragedy. The fire-and-brimstone, crusades faith of previous generations is not going to endure through the changes our culture is undergoing.

My hope is that the remaining contingent of faithful believers will continue to do the hard work of self-reflection and log-removing from our eyes, asking ourselves if what we say we believe is what we are truly living. We say we believe the gospel is for everyone—every wounded, confused, rough-around-the-edges sinner from every race, ethnicity, sexual orientation, and background—and I pray that the millennial church will embrace that principle, taking what we believe in theory and repenting for the ways in which we have historically failed to put it into practice.

REFLECTION QUESTIONS

- Why have you stayed in the church in spite of obstacles in your path?

- How does Kelsey's story of losing faith in the religious elite resonate with you?

- How might we work to be more transparent as the institutional church, both in form and practice?

Chapter 16

THE SACRED STORY

Millennials, Dying, Death, and Resurrection

*I believe in the Holy Spirit, the holy catholic church, the communion
of saints, the forgiveness of sins, the resurrection of the body, and the
life everlasting. Amen.* —*The Apostles' Creed*

When I first conceived this book and proposed it to my friends and colleagues, it didn't include a chapter like this. But as word got out that I was
writing the book, one day over lunch one of my mentors in ministry suggested that I talk about death and reenvisioning the way millennials look
at the last things: dying, death, and resurrection. If this book seeks to speak
the sacred story of death and resurrection to the institutional church, then
it must also speak the sacred story to the millennial generation as well.

I approach this chapter with some of my own millennial baggage.
Because I have seen the effects of death and experienced the toll of losing
someone, I too have a fear of death. But I trust the words of Paul in his first
letter to the church at Corinth when he writes,

> When this perishable body puts on imperishability, and this mortal body
> puts on immortality, then the saying that is written will be fulfilled: Death
> has been swallowed up in victory. Where, O death is your victory? Where,
> O death is your sting? The sting of death is sin, and the power of sin is
> the law. But thanks be to God, who gives us the victory through our Lord
> Jesus Christ. (1 Cor 15:54-57)

If God is who God says God is, then we can take God for God's word. We
have a strong and certain hope that death will be destroyed, so let's have a
frank conversation on living faithfully and dying with grace in our hearts.

Let's have a conversation with stained-glass millennials and millennials in general regarding the end of our earthly existence and the beginning of the hereafter.

The Millennial Problem with Death

Stanley Hauerwas, Gilbert T. Rowe Professor of Divinity and Law Emeritus at Duke Divinity School, said this about death:

> Death is one of the things that modern Christianity doesn't know how to deal with. . . . People say they want to die quickly, painlessly and in their sleep because they don't want to know they're dying. . . . In the Book of Common Prayer in the Great Litany there is the prayer, "Deliver us from lightening, tempest, from earthquake, fire, flood, from plague, pestilence and famine, Good Lord deliver us. From all oppression, conspiracy, rebellion, from violence, battle and murder, and from dying suddenly and unprepared." In the middle ages what people feared is what we want, a sudden death. And they feared a sudden death because they wanted to have time to be reconciled with God, their enemies (who were usually their families), and the church. They wanted to have a lingering death because what they feared was God and we just fear death. We just want to put it off. . . . I think that's been a part of what modern Christianity has been about, trying to help people think we're really not going to die.[1]

Millennial Christians have a problem with death because we have been raised to fear and prevent death instead of embracing it as part of the natural cycle of life. We have faced dying with the evolution and revolution of medical care and the decline of faith, so we have good reason to fear. We need only to look to Jesus, the pioneer of death and life abundant to see that he too felt anguish over death:

> To live in the knowledge that one is perfectly loved by God and that death no longer has the victory is not a way of denying death or an incitement to cover one's emotions and passions and live as if death is not painful. Jesus, the one who clearly loved God in all things and at all times and who had a deeper grasp of the meaning of death than anyone around him, is deeply troubled in the face of death than anyone around him, is deeply troubled in the face of the death of his friend [Lazarus].[2]

To that end, even Jesus asked that the cup of death he was facing be passed from him (Matt 26:39). But Jesus also accepted God's will and what was coming and went forth prepared to die as one who would go on to live. We need to reframe the way we talk about death for the sake of our lives. Our mode of speaking about death needs to shift from preventing death to extending the quality of our lives. Again, it is about being authentic and vulnerable. To speak about death, we must speak about what we believe about death authentically.

Dying into God

Recently, I attended a funeral with my grandmother, and we sat and reminisced about her friendship with the deceased. The service started, and all was well and good until we got to the point where, in my tradition, we say the Apostles' Creed: "I believe in the resurrection of the body and the life everlasting." I found myself pausing for a moment and grasping the reality of that statement. In the midst of death, we Christians were proclaiming life. In the midst of sadness, we were saying that sadness and mourning will not have a final say because we believe in the resurrection of the body.

After the funeral, my Nana was obviously grappling with losing her friend and dealing with her own mortality when we talked. I didn't know what to say to her. She's fifty years my senior, and frankly I was left speechless. I think we need to start speaking about death as a ministry to those whom stained-glass millennials will care for in their dying moments. We are on our way to a seismic dying of a generation in the church. People who are closer to death than most millennials are now need a good word, and the millennials who are dealing with those deaths need to be able to articulate the message of the gospel and talk about dying well in a constructive way.

How does that happen? Death must no longer be taboo in our congregations as some distant thing that will happen years from now. I'm not suggesting it should be ignored or, even worse, become the central message of a church. We don't need more "Sinners in the Hands of an Angry God" sermons. What we need are frank conversations about dying faithfully and going on to live with God.

Get Your Ash in Church

One way the church articulates that we are creatures and not Creators is by observing Ash Wednesday. We are the evidence and traces of the goodness of God because of our need for God. So when we have ashes imposed on our foreheads, we do so in the hope of God showing up to enable us to fix the mess we've made. But also, when we have ashes imposed on our foreheads, we remind ourselves that we will die. We, like billions of people before us, will face a time when we will be no more.

In that instance, we have two options. Either we face oblivion, the utter destruction of our very beings, by way of there being no God. Or we die into the love of God and become the Love that surrounds and envelops the entirety of creation. With all the doubts millennials (and frankly all of us) have about death and life hereafter, I am reminded of the words of the late theologian Marcus Borg, who wrote, "So, is there an afterlife, and if so, what will it be like? I don't have a clue. But I am confident that the one who has buoyed us up in life will also buoy us up through death. We die into God. What more that means, I do not know. But that is all I need to know."[3]

For us and for our salvation, we don't need half-truths or fleeting answers. What we need is a healthy dose of doubt mixed with faith mixed with hope. Nadia Bolz-Weber has a wonderful story about Ash Wednesday that illustrates my point:

> Here I was on Ash Wednesday, standing in a birthing room at the University of Colorado Hospital, on the day that the church remembers that we are but dust and to dust we will return. With one hand, I held a small metal pot of ashes and with the other, I reached across Duffy's recovery bed and made the sign of the cross with black ashes on her forehead, then on Charlie's too. Duffy had that beautiful and totally exhausted look of a woman who had just given birth, and Charlie had that proud and totally exhausted look of a partner who had just spent hours feeling helpless. "The baby too?" I then asked her parents. Duffy and Charlie said, "Yes, please, the baby too." My voice strained a bit as I pressed ever so gently into the brow of baby Willa's brand-new skin, flesh that had been exposed to air for only a few precious hours. I couldn't completely constrain the trembling in my voice as I reminded all of us in the room that even she, full of beauty and hope and just hours from her mother's womb, will, at her death, return to dust and the very heart of God. And the mother mouthed, "Thank you." And then I knew. I knew more than on any other Ash Wednesday that the promises of baptisms and funerals, the promises of birth and death, are inextricably wrapped up together. For we come from God and to God we shall go. There is so much that gets in the way of that simple truth.[4]

The reality is that we are born into love, live into love, and die into love. That's what millennials need to hear. And just as Ash Wednesday is not the end of the liturgical year, so too is dying not the end of the road for Christians. We must turn our attention to death itself: the Good Friday of our existence.

Death Itself

I remember the day like it was yesterday. It was the morning of Halloween, and I was scheduled to preach the next day to commemorate All Saints' Day. I received a call I had never imagined receiving at seventeen years old. My friend, Abbey, whom I mentioned in a previous chapter, had died. She was killed in a car accident. The whole community gasped as this laughing, joyous, beautiful sixteen-year-old had left this life far too soon. I remember one of my friends asking me where God was. I communicated my frustration to my grandfather that I didn't have an answer to that question. Luckily, my grandfather came to my aid. He had been writing poetry for years and wrote these words: "Where was God when Abbey died? He was right there by her side, he loved her, she was not alone, he held her close, he took her home."

The beauty of those short few lines of poetry isn't their elegance or grace in the face of a tragic situation. It's how they answer the questions we all long to know. Where was God? The answer is not that God initiated the death or caused it but that God was present in the midst of death. This points to what we know to be true about Jesus. Jesus did not choose to circumvent suffering and death. Instead, in spite of his hesitations, he went to face his destiny.

I think that millennials are more scared of death itself than of the dying process. We have combatted death with medical achievements and advancements, but we cannot stop it from happening. I'm reminded of the words of Emily Dickinson's well-known poem: "Because I could not stop for Death, he kindly stopped for me." In a fast-paced, fear-based culture, we see ourselves stopping finitely in death. In this culture hell-bent on prolonging life, what could be scarier than death?

We need to learn to die well. We need to learn language that will help us give voice to the reality that death is more friend than foe. We who have a sure and certain hope in the gospel of Jesus Christ know that death is not the end. That doesn't make it any easier, and it doesn't make it any less morbid. But death no longer has the power it once had. Death no longer has the final say. And it is in that reality that we can move forward to live in the great hereafter in the presence of the glorious saints of light. This brings us to the sacred story we Christians share across lines of denominations, viewpoints, and understandings: that of resurrection.

Resurrection

I love this line in the movie *A River Runs Through It*: "My father was very sure about certain matters pertaining to the universe. To him all good things—trout as well as eternal salvation—come by grace and grace comes by art and art does not come easy."[5] I think that Christians can appreciate, articulate, and celebrate talking about resurrection, for in resurrection we are promised that there is more authenticity to this life than one could ever hope for. There is more vulnerability, hope, peace, and joy than one could ever dream of. In resurrection, we see the fruition of God's eternal promise that God is not done with millennials, with baby boomers, with Gen X'ers and Gen Y'ers yet. And ultimately God will never be done with creation. God never gives up and God never fails. The hope of this sacred story is that, as the prophet James Taylor once sang, "We are bound and we are bound."[6] Friends, we are bound here and now for the sake of the kingdom, and we are bound then and there on a journey toward eternity. We are bound together for the kingdom of God, and we are bound for the kingdom of God.

I've always found myself waking up early to preach on Sundays. And those of you who know me know how incredibly difficult that is. But I'm starting to realize that there is something truly magnificent about being up "early on the first day of the week while it was still dark" (John 20:1). For that is when resurrection first happened, and it is where resurrection happens again and again every time the people of God gather to proclaim that death died that day long ago.

Resurrection in the millennial mindset should be an idea that has us working, waiting, and watching right now. My friend, the Reverend Michael Lea, taught me many things in my time as his assistant at First Baptist Church, but one of the most important was to beware of "religious certainty." He said he was always cautious of those who have it figured all out. To claim that we know for certain how the resurrection of the dead will occur is dangerous because it leaves no room for faith and hope. And without faith and hope, do we really have resurrection in the first place?

I honestly don't have all the answers when it comes to the resurrection of the body and the life everlasting. When I was a child, someone asked me what color carpet I would want in my heavenly mansion. I think that style of thinking about heaven is dated and frankly pedantic in the eyes of what eternity might be. As I've grown, I like to think of heaven more as an example of the Eucharist. We are brought together around a common table and given the feast meant for eternity. Fellowship, friendship, and communion with our Creator await us in the hereafter. We have no certitudes as to what that looks like, or the color of carpet in heaven, but I am hopeful that when I get there it will be wilder and grander than any human conception of heaven might be.

Millennials don't need certainty in their theology of resurrection. The church doesn't need certainty in its theology of resurrection. They don't need to be told who's in heaven and who's not (frankly, they've been told that their entire lives). What they do need to know is how to bring heaven here—how to pray the prayer, "Thy kingdom come, thy will be done on earth as it is in heaven," and really mean what they say when they ask for the kingdom of God to come here.

When I was at the Duke Youth Academy, one of our professors spoke to us about realized eschatology, the idea that humanity has the potential to play a role in bringing about the kingdom of God here and now. That's not to say that God can't do it by God's self, but God invites us into the divine dance of the cosmos. God invites us on our island home of earth to help bring forth the kingdom that God intends for the world. It's a place where peace and equality play a larger role than war and inequality, a place where people are uplifted for their differences and not torn down, a place where finest bread and wine are offered at Christ's table for all who seek it. If we can get that started, then the church will vanquish the rumors of its demise for the sake of something bigger than we could have possibly expected. The church will be resurrected.

Notes

1. "Stanley Hauerwas on Dying," available at https://relewis.wordpress.com/2010/05/26/stanley-hauerwas-on-dying/ (accessed 21 October 2016).

2. John Swinton and Richard Payne, eds., *Living Well and Dying Faithfully: Christian Practices for End-of-Life Care* (Grand Rapids MI: William B. Eerdmans Publishing Company, 2009).

3. Marcus Borg, *Speaking Christian: Why Christian Words Have Lost Their Meaning and Power—And How They Can Be Restored* (San Francisco: HarperOne, 2011).

4. Nadia Bolz-Weber, excerpt from *Accidental Saints*, available at http://www.patheos.com/blogs/nadiabolzweber/2016/02/a-little-reading-for-fat-tuesdayash-wednesday-from-accidental-saints/ (accessed 21 October 2016).

5. *A River Runs Through It*, dir. Robert Redford, Allied Filmmakers, 1992.

6. James Taylor, "Shed a Little Light," *New Moon Shine*, 1991.

Chapter 17

REFLECTIONS FROM THE STAINED GLASS

with The Reverend Sarah Heath

Though parts of the movement may be slowing down, if being a person of faith has taught me anything it's that there must be death to have resurrection, and perhaps we are in a season of pruning.
—*Sarah Heath*

Sarah Heath is a pastor in the United Methodist Church in Southern California. She is originally from Canada, but she and her family moved to Mississippi when she was a teenager. She has contributed to *Sojourners* and famously appeared on an episode of *Chuck Knows Church,* a popular Christian YouTube series on the ecclesial ins-and-outs of participating in the life of the church. Sarah is a witness to the idea that God calls those who may not initially want to experience a call to ministry. As you will read in her story, she has continually said "yes" to God's invitation on her life.

The Reverend Sarah Heath received her BA in psychology from the University of Southern Mississippi and her MDiv from Duke University Divinity School. A Canadian native, she is a well known writer and speaker.

Rob Lee: Tell me how you were called to the ministry.

Sarah Heath: I didn't grow up wanting to be a pastor. It wasn't that being a woman stopped me from seeing that as a career; my faith had been deeply influenced by the female pastor who had led my confirmation class. She told my parents after confirmation that our faith was up to us, and should our parents drag us to church, she would talk to them. She believed our faith was a choice that we were making for ourselves once we were confirmed. I was blown away! Suddenly, the faith was up to me, and I never stopped choosing it from that class forward.

I grew up in Canada but moved to Mississippi at age fourteen, and it was at this age that we started attending the denomination in which I am now an ordained Elder. I had been attending a summer camp every summer from the time I was five. It was an Inter-Varsity camp back in Canada, and at seventeen I did a program called Leader in Training. It was the first time I saw myself as a leader in a faith setting. I still wasn't thinking full-time ministry was anything I wanted to do. In college I studied biology and psychology. I was busy with a full plate that included my campus ministries, on-campus recreational sports, a heavy course load, and a sorority, but I still volunteered with a local youth group. There I found that all my interests and hobbies that didn't seem to go together were ways I could relate to different students and provided a great starting point for us. I realized that if I could do anything with my time, it was share my faith with these students and journey with them. As busy as I was, I always had time for them. I couldn't imagine anything being more fulfilling.

On a beach retreat with one of my campus ministries, I shared with the campus minister that I felt called into ministry. She looked at me and said, "Thank goodness. We have all been waiting for you to see the call the rest of us have always seen." It was confirmation that folks saw in me what I hadn't yet seen in myself. I still wasn't sure about being in ministry, so I kind of challenged God by applying to only one seminary and only a seminary that was notorious for being hard to get into. I was blessed not only to get in but also to have financial help so I could afford it. I guess you could say I had no choice at that point!

Why buy stock in a dying organization? That is to say, why are you pursuing a calling that many millennials and people your age have given up?

Truthfully, I ask myself this question daily. Is what I am doing the best use of my time and the best way to bring people to reconciliation and wholeness? On bad days I think there are one hundred other ways I could help people, and probably with less bureaucracy and in places where people wouldn't be as difficult. But there are good days and even great days when I know that God transforms all things. Within local church communities, there seems to be a particularly great environment for growth. I have seen amazing things, and I myself wouldn't be who I am without being formed by a local church community.

I also know that being a pastor is a vocation, and no matter what I do I will always have this calling on my life, so even if church as it is currently no longer exists, I will be doing ministry in some form. Even if I were a bartender, barista, artist, speaker, actress, doctor, vet, or in another career I have ever thought of, part of me knows I would still be leading a Bible study somewhere and meeting with people to share coffee, conversation, and kingdom questions. It's who I am, not just what I do.

How has your calling affected your relationships, friendships, and family dynamics? Are they concerned that you're interested in a precarious ministry? What is your response to them?

That's a tough question. I am not married, and sometimes I know one of the reasons is that I have been married to my job and I keep a different schedule than my friends and peers. I don't get to live the "normal" life of many of my millennial friends. I have missed every camping trip, fun weekend wine tasting, Sunday race days, and all the other events where most of my friends met their significant others. I think, honestly, most of my friends outside the church don't really get my job. I always hear, "I have never met a pastor/minister/priest like you." I usually laugh and say that's the point. God uses me to reach people who may be disarmed by meeting me and not your "typical" pastor. Another of my responses is, "I know it isn't the standard career, but a deep part of me is a storyteller, and my favorite narrative is the one of God's love for God's people. I would be telling this story and sharing Christ's love no matter what I do, so at least for now I get paid for it!"

Where have you seen God in the millennial generation?

I think it is interesting that many think the millennial generation is the "me" generation, and I think that with all the social media available, it does seem that we are more aware of ourselves and our perceived images than previous generations, but I have also seen amazing things come out of that. From global movements to end slavery to people using Twitter to encourage others, I think God is using the "smallness" of the current world to be able to create a global movement and connection. Even with all the global connection, I am also starting to see people meet face to face again.

I have a favorite coffee shop I go to, and I always see groups of people my age and younger meeting and discussing the Bible or something equally faith related. As we have more and more information at our fingertips and in our pockets, I think we are claiming parts of our faith for ourselves and researching for ourselves. People don't want to hear what the perceived authority figure has to say; they want to participate and be part of a movement. They don't just want to hear about the kingdom of God; they want to act it out. They are part of the "do it yourself" artisan generation. They want to create and participate, not just consume. It makes me think of the scene in *Good Will Hunting* where Will is having an argument with students from an expensive Ivy League school about intelligence, and he shares that everything he learned was available with his $10.00 library card. Maybe now learning starts with websites like Buzzfeed, but with any luck people will dig deeper and journey and learn together.

What gives you the most hope about the church?

I was recently meeting with a group of people from the millennial generation (or were a little older) about a church-planting situation, and I asked if they could have anything in a church, what would they want. I was surprised when they wanted a church that was progressive in social action but orthodox in belief about Christ. They didn't want a mega-church atmosphere. They wanted to be together with people of various ages, wrestling with their faith. I wanted to create something catchy, something gimmicky, and it was them who said, "No. We want church." Millennials want to know why people do the things they do, why tradition matters, and how it applies to them. They want to hear the same narratives that the church has always shared, but they want to be able to engage it in many different ways, from art to liturgy. I was surprised to hear them say these things. It sounds funny, but they gave me hope. It isn't that the story doesn't matter anymore or that traditions aren't important; it is that how we tell the story must be compelling and informative and affect people's daily lives.

Why stay? Why now? Why be a part of this movement that is slowing down?

Again this is a conversation I have with myself a lot, especially when a friend of mine points out, "Sarah, all the skills that make you successful at ministry would make you a lot of money in the private sector"; this is tempting when at my age I still have a roommate. But I know that I wouldn't be as fulfilled doing anything else right now—though parts of the movement may be slowing down, if being a person of faith has taught me anything it's that there must be death to have resurrection, and perhaps we are in a season of pruning. I want to be a part of what is going to be birthed next. Why now? I can only say because this is the unique time of life when I get to be in the world. This is it, my one life, so I think this is a great time to be part of something beyond myself.

What are your hopes for the future of the institutional church?

I hope that we will not cling too tightly to things and intstead allow the Spirit to move in whatever way it will move. The Spirit will continue to transform lives and have people excited to be their most authentic selves before God, but we may miss out on partnering in that.

I hope we make it less hierarchical so that more people can participate in leadership. The United Methodist ordination process weeds out some amazing entrepreneurial types who would help the church in such amazing ways. Why go through all the hoops when an artisan just wants to get to the outcome and so creates a church with a denomination that has fewer hoops or with no denomination at all?

REFLECTION QUESTIONS

- In what ways have you responded to God's invitation with a resounding *yes*?
- In what ways has your denomination weeded out people who may be qualified to do ministry?
- How might God be calling you to ministry?

Chapter 18

ENGAGING MILLENNIALS

A Guide for Everyone Else

I love to tell the story, 'twill be my theme in glory, to tell the old, old story of Jesus and his love. —Katherine Hankey[1]

Jean-Luc Picard, captain of the *Starship Enterprise* in *Star Trek: The Next Generation*, is famous for getting the crew moving to their destination by saying one simple word: "engage." What I would give to have one word to get the church moving! But, alas, we are left without a singular word, phrase, or idea to get the church to engage with itself and others. This chapter seeks to create a tapestry of how to engage with stained-glass millennials in your context and setting.

Throughout this chapter, it is my hope that you will see your own story linked to that of the millennial generation. For in our stories we have hope. The main intersection of community happens in our stories, where we see commonalities and traces of hope. In our stories, we have the hope of the resurrecting power of God. If God can make the story of Christ beautiful, what could God do to your story? May your engagement with millennials be in the same spirit that God has engaged us: full of grace, truth, and hope.

Engaging in a Reteaching of Loveliness

My mentor and friend Nathan Kirkpatrick often reminds me of a line from Galway Kinnell: "Sometimes it is necessary to reteach a thing its loveliness."[2] I feel like there are no truer words for millennials. The church needs to remind my generation of its loveliness in the twenty-first century. Never has a generation in recent memory been ostracized by the church more than millennials. There is a tendency for the church to condemn what it cannot explain. There is a tendency in the church today to condemn the realities and complexities of the millennial generation.

If we're honest with ourselves, we will admit that this reaction and condemnation is born out of fear. The church is afraid that it is losing its footing. The stronghold of the church is not what it used to be. I'm just as scared as everyone else about the future, but that doesn't negate the present work we are called to do here and now for the sake of then and there. We are called to be faithful to all generations. This calling includes an engagement with millennials.

Truly, millennials are desperate for a good word that comes from the church of Jesus Christ, and that word can take the form of a smile when a millennial enters a church instead of a glare. It could come in the form of a theological conversation over coffee that enables questions instead of shying away from them. But I must be frank and say that if you want to have a conversation with a millennial, then you must be willing to go deep into the realm of questioning, doubt, and faith. Millennials don't need platitudes; they need the good news that the church and its people do not have it all figured out.

If God's people are not certain, then we are free to discuss our questions openly. Certainty is dangerous when you want to engage millennials. The simplicity of certainty isn't appealing to the generation that questions everything. Perhaps that is one of God's greatest gifts to the church from millennials: we can no longer hold on to theological certainties or platitudes. We must faithfully engage God in ways that require authenticity.

Moving Beyond Platitudes

Moving beyond platitudes requires that we be true to ourselves and true to God. In this endeavor, we must abandon theological ideas and phrases that ignore who God is. We've all heard phrases or buzzwords that seek to paint an image of God with broad strokes while leaving out the subtleties of what we know about God. How many times have we heard the phrases, "God needed another angel in heaven" or "Love the sinner, hate the sin," and then proceeded to listen to a pitiful excuse for theological understanding? If you've heard these phrases and cringed, you can be certain millennials have as well.

If we're serious about this church business, then we must be willing to acknowledge that the church hasn't always had the corner on what to say and how to say it. In our efforts to become relevant and always to have something to say, we have forgotten the beauty of mystery. The Trinitarian mystery that we claim as believers in God—Father, Son, and Holy Spirit— is one of the most radical claims the world has seen these many years. But it is crazy enough to be believable. What kind of God would come down and walk among Creation? The God we have come to know in Christ—a God who has made it God's business to be for and with us. And if God is for us and with us, who can be against us (see Rom 8)?

Deeper than that, I'm reminded of the song "I Will Arise and Go to Jesus." In that iconic hymn, we hear the words, "if you tarry till you're better, you will never come at all." If the church seeks to have it all figured out and not embrace the mystery of our God, we may never figure it out. The whole idea of gaining a grasp of God or God's will or God's mind isn't conducive to the gospel of Jesus Christ. That being said, we catch glimpses not only of God's will and God's mind but also of God's heart. In that heart, we see that God has held all of humanity and creation since before we could come up with platitudes.

In our own context, it is important in our engagement with millennials to share the news of this great God. I remember seeing Garrison Keillor at my alma mater, Appalachian State University. He remarked that he was afraid Americans would forget the songs we've been taught since we were little because future generations will have technology to occupy their time. He wondered if in fifty years we'll know songs like "Shenandoah," "Home on the Range," or other iconic American songs. I, too, echo that question, but from a faith perspective. Countless families are now in the second generation of "nones," and that means they have no recollection of the hymns, songs, and stories that we know to be true about God and that speak to the great news of God. How are you going to remind generations younger than you of the song in the heart of God?

If you're not careful, you may be singing to yourself before long. I can't stress enough the importance of authentic engagement with millennials. I speak for my generation when I say we are desperate for conversation partners. Millennials just want a chance to shine and be a part of the great conversation of faith.

Engaging Millennials in Pentecost

Pentecost was the moment when the Holy Spirit descended and rested on mortal bodies. For many biblical scholars, it is the completion of the Tower of Babel, in which God became available again to the multitudes. God, once dispelling humanity's ability to connect through language due to the fall, reconnect the fledgling church through Christ to to the reality of shared language by the gift of Pentecost. I feel as if we can learn something from the fruition of Pentecost.

Millennials need to hear God in their own language: the language that acknowledges they are valued and have sacred worth in the eyes of God and in the eyes of the church. For too long the church has tried to silence millennial voices in their contexts instead of engaging them. I once sat in a class on millennials in the church and heard someone ask, "How do we start a worship service for millennials?" I feel like that is missing the point. We're not trying to lure millennials back with flashy worship or by catering to them and their tastes. They actually want quite the opposite. An authentic engagement with millennial Christians and non-Christians alike requires a realization of where one is standing. That is, we, the church, must first acknowledge our own issues before we begin to engage in healthy and fruitful conversations with millennials.

That requires careful, meticulous soul searching. It requires the church to acknowledge and admit that we don't have the monopoly the church once did in ages past. In that realization, we can begin to heal the broken bridge to the millennial generation. To engage a millennial in conversation on the nature of the church or theology is to be a participant in the re-creation of Pentecost.

What Millennials Don't Need

It seems like every church consultant has a list of ideas that would work to engage millennials. This generation is the "buzzword" right now. People think if you can convince a millennial to come to church, you must be doing something right. Let me offer this advice: avoid that mentality at all costs. The hope-filled, Spirit-moving, life-giving church we have come to know is as authentic and real as it gets. When we begin to cater to millennials, we are like the great-aunt who just started using Facebook for the first time: we simply don't know or understand how the reality of the faith community works. For the church to relearn its inherent loveliness, it must start by acknowledging that engagement with young generations is weak.

Think of it this way: I know my gifts and graces are in ministering to God's people. For me to attempt to be anything else wouldn't be authentic. In the same way, the church must acknowledge its strengths while not overlooking its growing edges. The church has to be authentic while pushing forward into the future. If we fail to do that, then we've lost more than just millennials. We will lose future generations as well.

"How do we start a worship service for millennials?" The moment I heard this question, I knew the person would never reach a single millennial without some serious work on what it means to engage people in the twenty-first century. To be the church today, we must consider new and different ways to reach and engage the generation who will define this century. We must be willing to push and prod this old church into new and different ways of ministering in the world for the transformation of disciples.

Turn the Page

In an episode of *Star Trek: The Next Generation*, Captain Jean-Luc Picard faces the greatest villains the series ever created: the half-cyborg, half-organic beings known as the Borg. Captain Picard is touring his ship as the captains of old did before battle, and one of his counterparts asks him if he expects to prevail. He responds, "We may yet prevail. That's a conceit. But it's a healthy one. I wonder if the Emperor Honorius watching the Visigoths coming over the seventh hill truly realized that the Roman Empire was about to fall. This is just another page in history, isn't it? Will this be the end of our civilization? Turn the page."[3]

The church is at the same juncture. Will this be the end? Will our engagement (or failure to engage) with one another be the end of the institutional church? We have no way of knowing beyond trusting Christ's promise to be with us to the end of the age. I for one am confident that the church will be around until Christ brings all things to completion in the day of our Lord. Even so, we cannot be complacent, we cannot fall back, and we cannot stop now. We must continue to engage one another in beautiful ways; in the end, we are the ones who turn the page.

Notes

1. Katherine Hankey, "I Love to Tell the Story," c. 1868.

2. Galway Kinnell, "Saint Francis and the Sow," available at http://www.poetryfoundation.org/poems-and-poets/poems/detail/42683 (accessed 22 October 2016).

3. "The Best of Both Worlds: Part I," *Star Trek: The Next Generation,* 1990.

Chapter 19

CONCLUSION

Everything dies, baby, that's a fact, but maybe everything that dies someday comes back. —*Bruce Springsteen*[1]

In the twenty-first century, the church faces a bleak reality, yet I still have hope. I have hope after hearing these stories and listening to the people who choose to be a part of the church even amid the landscape of what some call a post-Christian culture. I have hope because ultimately we are a resurrection people, clinging to the resiliency and tradition of the past and looking to the future.

I'm a firm believer that for millennials to carry forward the banner of Christianity, the church as a whole is going to have to ask the hard questions. Do we want to survive? Do we want to continue in vibrant ministry and healthy worship? If the answer is yes, then we're going to need more stories like we've heard in this book. We're going to need church people to overinvest in the youth of the world. In his poem *Ulysses*, Alfred Tennyson has these words:

> Tho' much is taken, much abides; and tho'
> We are not now that strength which in old days
> Moved earth and heaven, that which we are, we are;
> One equal temper of heroic hearts,
> Made weak by time and fate, but strong in will
> To strive, to seek, to find, and not to yield.[2]

Though much is taken, much abides. Though we moved heaven and earth in ages past, we are weak by time and fate. The church isn't what it used to be. But the church, for the sake of the gospel, cannot yield. We cannot give up because the salvation of humanity rests on the Jesus we worship, and it is our job to share the story of Jesus.

I remember growing up in a church where we'd have to pull out extra chairs on Christmas Eve and Easter. That reality is often no longer the case. But if we yield now, if we give up for the sake of numbers in our pews, then we fail not only the church but also the Lord of the church. Millennials need to experience Jesus of Nazareth in the ways that people before them experienced him.

If we are going to be the church, we have to remember that our place is no longer on the forefront of society but on the margins with the millennials and others who feel disenfranchised by the church. For us and for our future, we must find hope in the generation we have lost. We do that by telling the sacred stories we know, by believing in millennials and their sacred worth, by getting back to the basics.

In earlier chapters, I mentioned that in Acts 2, after the Pentecost account, the first church devoted themselves to sharing prayers in the temple, sharing their possessions, and breaking bread together. God added to their number of converts daily because of their faithfulness (Acts 2:46-47). If we want to reclaim the millennial generation for the church and for Christ, we must get back to the basics of breaking bread and praying together. Millennials crave the simplicity of the liturgy we once knew. I've heard time and again that my generation doesn't need a laser rock show for church; they need to hear that they are loved by a community and by God for their sacred and intrinsic worth.

For the church and for the future, we must hear and tell stories like those in this book in an effort to show that God is not done with us yet. God has a future for the church because God is full of resurrecting power. In that hope, the church moves forward through the ages.

I was once asked why I have such an ardent belief that the future of the church has the potential to be bright in spite of all the church faces. My answer is simple: resurrection. God is all about resurrection; God is all about bringing a glorious Easter morning out of the terror of crucifixion. Simply and directly, the twenty-first-century church is waiting on the Easter morning of its existence. If God could bring to life Jesus in first-century Palestine, couldn't God bring to life the institution of the church in the twenty-first century?

If God is a God of resurrection, then the worst thing that can happen to a church isn't decline or death. The worst thing that can happen is apathy to a hurting and broken world. When I was ordained in the Cooperative

Baptist Fellowship, the Reverend Nathan Kirkpatrick reminded me and those present that I was suddenly accountable to our world in a new way. Let this book be an ordination for you. After reading these pages, you are accountable to the millennial generation in a new way.

Some of you might feel daunted, but there is such hope in the reality of being accountable to a generation in a new way. One of the many examples of hope in our time is found in scenes of resurrection among millennials. Vibrant, intergenerational churches across the religious landscape are working with and for the resurrection of a generation. Stained-glass millennials are committed to the future of the church, and that is a beautiful thing. In that spirit, we pray for another Great Awakening amid a generation that has such gifts and graces for ministry. The reality is that millennials who stay in the church cannot complete this mission by themselves. They need the help of generations that have gone before them. They need the resurrecting power that each generation has experienced since Christ's institution of the church.

As I reflect on the stories of my colleagues and friends who choose to stay in the institutional church, I am filled with peace. My grandmother often reminded me that the church is always a generation away from extinction. I have confidence that this is not the generation that will bury the church; we have strong leaders and confident laity who will move the church further into the twenty-first century.

In conclusion, the hope of the future is based on the expression of Jesus Christ in these stained-glass millennials—people who are willing to stay and fight for what they know to be true about God and the church. In story after story, faithful people have taken up the banner and planted themselves in what they knew to be true about God. As I finish this book, I am sitting in the Divinity School on the campus of Duke University, a place that has given me so much. I can't help feeling thankful that there are other people across this country who are willing and able to attend divinity school and seminary.

We need millennial leaders who are willing to take up the cross of the church and carry it well into the future. In our time and our place, how will our story be committed to history? Will we be the people who put the nails on the coffin of the church, or will we be the people who run to the tomb, hoping to meet a risen Jesus there? These are questions left for my generation. This is the occasion we must rise to. May we, like Mary, Peter, and John, go to the tomb with trepidation and perhaps a strong eternal hope. Thanks be to God. Amen.

Notes

1. Bruce Springsteen, "Atlantic City," *Nebraska*, 1982.

2. Alfred, Lord Tennyson, *Ulysses*, available at http://www.poetryfoundation.org/poem/174659.

AFTERWORD

Holy Spirit, breathe on me until my heart is clean let sunshine fill its inmost parts with not a cloud between. Breathe on me, breathe on me, Holy Spirit, breathe on me! Take thou my hearth, cleanse every part. Holy Spirit, breathe on me.[1]

In Paul's farewell tour in Acts 20, he stops by the village of Troas to preach to the converts again. Luke draws back the curtains on an early congregation and allows us to peer into their life together. They meet at night; they eat; they have at least one person in the youth group. His name is "Eutychus." In Greek, his name means (appropriately) "lucky."

The book of Acts features characters who are at midlife or older. Many of them are recovering from their past before the resurrection. They are growing older and trying to follow the Spirit's leading through open doors. Only a handful of people could be classified as college students or adolescents. John Mark, Eutychus, and Timothy comprise the very small group of young people, and two of them have questionable reputations. John Mark is the first dropout from the mission field, and Eutychus is the first person to fall out of an upstairs window during a church service. If Acts had millennials, these three guys would be the ones. To follow Rob Lee's metaphor of the stained glass, Eutychus is the millennial who fell out of the window.

Eutychus drifts off in a state of sleep much like Samson or Jonah do. In the Bible, some people rest because of Sabbath; others sleep to avoid a situation or disobey.[2] Eutychus is in the latter category. He knows better. An ancient sermon would be difficult to sleep through. Most people responded to everything a speaker said. They interrupted, stomped their feet, applauded, and laughed. If you fell asleep, you were saying publicly, "I reject the message."

The church had a problem, however. Eutychus's behavior was as much of a concern to them as it was to him. As Charles Talbert explains in *Reading Acts,* the ancient world suspected that the Christians engaged in child sacrifice and drinking blood. After all, they worshiped a man who told them to eat his body and drink his blood. Losing a young person out of an upstairs window would only lead to the possibility of scandal.

Taking matters into his own hands, Paul stops his sermon, rushes to aid Eutychus, and revives the boy. He says, "Do not be alarmed, for his life is in him."

The reaction by the congregation is just as fascinating. They do not join Paul outside. They wait until the restoration is complete. They don't panic. When Eutychus returns, they feed him. They show him hospitality without retribution. Paul continues preaching. God gives the people comfort, and they finish the adventure.

I've often wondered what happened to Eutychus. Presumably, he helped write the next chapter for the church in Troas. He was certainly the luckiest guy in the book of Acts. Eutychus's story is a parable for the twenty-first-century church's relationship today with millennials.

Like Eutychus, many millennials have either fallen asleep or fallen out of what we call church today. Despite our best attempts to figure out, study, chronicle, depict, build programs for, teach, and develop this generation, we have not been able to stem the tide of something that is a sociological reality. Many people who grew up in the church at the turn of the twenty-first century are no longer in their congregations or denominations of origin. We read the statistics, we look around the pews, and we begin to think that we are like the church in Troas. We are scandalized by what we have done (or not done) to reach this generation.

Admittedly, the church has not made it easy on millennials. Any viewer of the movie *Spotlight* shudders at the sexual abuse that has happened in Jesus's name. We live with a church that is still recovering from the culture wars, worship divisions, and customized camps and programs of the 1970s, '80s, and '90s. The church growth movement of the 1970s laid the groundwork for the program church of the 1980s and 1990s. In our attempts to reach youth, we marginalized them. Youth ministries customized around music and programming for students segregated adolescents from the larger church and created churches focused on meeting individual needs rather than inviting people to a life on mission for Christ.

Stained-Glass Millennials gives us a counter-narrative to tell the church. Through testimony and analysis, Rob Lee has reminded us that what we see or perceive is not completely true. These millennials are actually still the church. They have been revived and restored by witnessing the presence of the risen Christ in individuals who are modern-day apostle Pauls. They are willing to interrupt church as we know it, follow others through their darkness, and revive today's Eutychus. Through friendships with individuals who have stayed with them, loved them, and restored them to the fellowship, they joined existing churches.

Of course, many church leaders, more concerned about finances or perception in the community, have behaved more like Sapphira, Herod Agrippa, or the priest Ananias. Denominations and churches have reacted to the perceived loss of "young people" and the decline in church attendance by working on everything but reviving Eutychus.

While the church of the late twentieth century was "focusing on the family," the millennials were born into a world where half of the families were falling apart. While pastors, youth ministers, and musicians fought over the number of times to sing the chorus of a song or whether to start a service "for the young people," millennials found refuge in parachurch organizations like Young Life, Fellowship of Christian Athletes, and Campus Crusade. While churches sent money and pooled their funds to help denominations maintain their brands and institutional headquarters, millennials awakened to God's call. While mainline and Baptist denominations took steps to begin new groups that would preserve the identity of their forebears, millennials looked past the brands and turned to Jesus and the relationships with people who behaved like Jesus. While many downtown churches fled cities or preserved the majority-white culture of their congregations, communities of faith were birthed with the understanding that "in Christ, there is neither Jew nor Greek, slave nor free, male nor female" (Gal 3:28). They bypassed traditional faith-based organizations and did what the Nike commercial instructed them: "Just do it."

But churches have never been perfect. We get things right and wrong. We are often mean to each other, and we do better on mission trips in other countries than we do with our neighbors next door. Out of our brokenness and confession can come a renewal of the church and the redemption of our world.

Christian millennials are leading these efforts. This generation continues to come back to the church, and older generations are beginning to recognize that we need their version of church. Despite the dire predictions that young people are leaving church, this book reminds us that the church—much like the kingdom of God—often works like yeast in dough. Millennials aren't going away, but it's highly unlikely that the church of yesterday will be able to count on their attendance or their giving the same way. Instead of coming to the church, they *are* the church.

Millennials don't fit into neat sociological categories. Their preferences alone have shaped everything from how we listen to music to how we order coffee at Starbucks. They come from every kind of family imaginable. Half of them have parents who divorced. Many of them have grown up under more than one roof. Even if their families have stayed intact, their friends' households have not. They have prepared us for a world where we don't just talk about "my parents"; we talk about "all the parents." We should not try to figure them out based on their choices or the perceived trends. Instead, like good disciples, we should learn from them.

Rob Lee and those interviewed here give me hope. I feel a bit like the apostle Paul must have felt when he told the Philippians that God is still doing a great work and will be faithful to complete it until the day of Christ Jesus (Phil 1:6). Millennials have largely resisted the siren calls of career paths, partly because the career dreams of their parents were not theirs, and because the promises that our culture has made to them went unfulfilled after 9/11/2001 and 9/11/2008. We have entrusted to them a world that will be recovering from perpetual war, climate problems, and economic instability. Those featured in this book have chosen to be the church, and the church has chosen to stay with them. Millennials have been willing to move into urban areas, restore cities, and reconcile people to Jesus when others have run from trauma.

In 2012, I visited a ninth grade English class in Baltimore. My nephew, Vincent Andrews, was teaching fifteen students basic writing skills. He was there on assignment from Teach for America. As in any other class, the students listened, disrupted, interrupted, and learned. Vincent did the best he could as a new teacher. He loved the students and worked hard for them. He ate a quick lunch at his desk each day and lost about twenty pounds. He took on more classes in the summer so that he could assist the students and their parents. Not all teachers would do that, but Vincent did. He brought some of the qualities that set millennials apart from previous generations: courage, passion, and resourcefulness. He answered a call to take on some of the deepest challenges left by previous generations. He's still in Baltimore because of the condition of the city and the problems he encountered. Instead of running from the problems, he's staying there to try to solve them. Other millennials have answered a call to war. Still others, like those featured in *Stained-Glass Millennials*, have answered Christ's call to his church.

Now the church can respond to what Christ is doing with and through millennials. If a church in Troas can break bread, welcome, and respond to resurrection, so can the church today. Eutychus is being revived and restored, and we're the lucky ones. Christ's presence goes before us into this generation and those who are following behind them. Our job as the church is to use the tools of hospitality—breaking bread, friendship, the table. Instead of welcoming millennials into the church (as Troas did for Eutychus), our role is to humble ourselves and to allow the millennials like Eutychus to welcome us. We wake up to Christ's presence in them. We join this generation that is answering God's call and follow them into the hardest, most difficult places. We respond to their invitation. They've been resurrected; we allow the risen Christ to breathe new life into us together. As the people of Troas discovered, we will be "not a little comforted" (Acts 20:12).

—Reverend Dr. William Shiell
President, Northern Seminary

Notes

1. "Breathe on Me," words by Edwin Hatch, adapt. and music by B. B. McKinney, 1937.

2. Charles Talbert, *Reading Acts: A Literary and Theological Commentary on the Acts of the Apostles,* Reading the New Testament Series (New York: Crossroad Publishing Company, 1997) 184–85.

70422383R00089

Made in the USA
San Bernardino, CA
01 March 2018